TRANSFORMATIVE ASEAN:

An Insider's Reflections

Pushpanathan Sundram

Jakarta, Indonesia

Transformative ASEAN: An Insider's Reflections
By Pushpanathan Sundram

For permissions and inquiries, please contact:
Gedung Menara Astra 37/F
Jl Jendral Sudirman Kav 5-6,
Jakarta Pusat 10220, Indonesia
Email: publish@ppaa.co
Website: www.ppaapublishing.com

PT Perkasa Permata Asia Abadi (PPAA), established in 2022 in Jakarta, Indonesia, publishes fiction and nonfiction. Dedicated to supporting emerging writers, we produce academic and creative works in English and major regional languages, fostering a vibrant literary community across Asia and beyond.

ISBN: 978-623-10-5605-4 (hardcover)
ISBN: 978-623-10-5604-7 (softcover)
ISBN: 978-623-10-5603-0 (e-book/PDF)

Published by: PT Perkasa Permata Asia Abadi (PPAA)
First Edition, 2024

Cover Design: Regina Rafika & Davya Daneilla

To the Secretaries-General of ASEAN, I had the honour of serving from 1997 to 2011: Tan Sri Ajit Singh, Mr. Ong Keng Yong, and the late Mr. Rodolfo Severino and Dr. Surin Pitsuwan.

Each of you has profoundly shaped my understanding of regional diplomacy and cooperation, imparting invaluable lessons in leadership, collaboration, and vision. This book is dedicated to your enduring legacy and profound influence on my life and career, which has guided me to navigate challenges and embrace opportunities with purpose and resolve.

Testimonials

Pushpanathan Sundram's Transformative ASEAN: An Insider's Reflections offers a deeply insightful account of ASEAN's evolution and impact, covering the political-security, economic and finance, socio-cultural and external relations dimensions through the last five decades. During my tenure as the Secretary-General of ASEAN, I witnessed his utmost dedication to ASEAN and strategic expertise in action as my Special Assistant and later Assistant Director/Head of External Relations. This book is his remarkable contribution, capturing ASEAN's extraordinary journey and its enduring significance in today's uncertain world.

- ***Tan Sri Ajit Singh, Secretary-General of ASEAN (1993-1997).***

This book comprehensively covers ASEAN's history and current realities. Drawing on his extensive insider insights and assessments, Pushpanathan offers a unique institutional perspective on the region's complexities and dynamics. It is a must-read for anyone who wants to understand ASEAN's past, present, and future.

- **Dr. Aladdin D. Rillo, Deputy Secretary General for the ASEAN Economic Community (2018-2021).**

Pushpanathan's book captures ASEAN's amazing transformation since its establishment in 1967 to maintain its relevance in a changing world. Drawing on his vast experience as the former ASEAN Deputy Secretary General, he provides fresh perspectives into ASEAN's enduring role in safeguarding peace, fostering regional cooperation, and advancing multilateralism in Southeast Asia.

- **Dato Dr. Ilango Karuppannian, Ambassador of Malaysia to Lebanon (2010-2014) and High Commissioner of Malaysia to Singapore (2016-2017).**

I not only had excellent working relations with the author during our memorable tenure as Deputy Secretaries-General in ASEAN but also witnessed the quality of his leadership and performance. His continued and deep engagement in ASEAN affairs after he left became a great human asset, providing one of the most valuable analytical insights into ASEAN's remarkable journey and significant achievements. I firmly believe that those who are keen to learn about ASEAN should not miss this book, Transformative ASEAN: An Insider's Reflections.

- **Mr. Sayakane Sisouvong, Deputy Secretary General for the ASEAN Political and Security Community (2009-2012).**

Pushpanathan, who has spent his career navigating this fascinating region, offers a valuable, comprehensive tour of ASEAN's history, its evolution and transformation. This is essential reading for anyone who wants to understand the region - not just its past but the important signposts the book offers to its future at a time of geopolitical uncertainty.

- **Ms. Penny Burt, Deputy High Commissioner of Australia to Singapore (2006-2010).**

ASEAN has achieved remarkable milestones and is a cornerstone of regional stability and collaboration. This book, written by an intellectual insider with firsthand experience, offers invaluable insights into ASEAN's successes and lessons learned. It is an essential read for understanding the factors shaping its transformative role in Southeast Asia and beyond.

- **Prof. Ora-orn Poocharoen, Founding Director, School of Public Policy, Chiang Mai University, Thailand.**

Transformative ASEAN: An Insider's Reflections adds an important contribution to the body of literature on the growing importance of middle-power nations in the world today. Pushpanathan's exploration of how ten diverse Southeast Asian nations have strategically leveraged their own vision and 'ASEAN Way' of using various forms of regional economic cooperation and integration to pursue their respective national interests offers tangible insights into how, since the 1997 Asian Financial Crisis and the COVID-19 pandemic, ASEAN has become Asia's premier regional economic hub and one of the global economy's most competitive destinations for international trade and foreign direct investment."

- **Mr. Marc Mealy, Chief Policy Officer & Senior Vice President, US-ASEAN Business Council.**

Acknowledgements

The insights and reflections shared in The Transformative ASEAN: An Insider's Reflections are profoundly influenced by my time as a staff member of the ASEAN Secretariat from 1997 to 2011. I owe a deep debt of gratitude to the Secretaries-General of ASEAN during this period, whose leadership and commitment to the organisation's vision were instrumental in shaping ASEAN's transformative journey. Their guidance and strategic foresight provided the foundation for many of ASEAN's achievements during this crucial era.

I extend my heartfelt appreciation to all my colleagues at the ASEAN Secretariat, including the support staff in Indonesia, whose dedication, hard work, and behind-the-scenes efforts often went unnoticed but were critical to ASEAN's success. The Secretariat staff's collective dedication to the ideals of regionalism and their unwavering belief in ASEAN's mission was a constant source of inspiration. Their teamwork, professionalism, and commitment to fostering regional cooperation made every challenge surmountable and every achievement meaningful.

I am deeply thankful to the ASEAN Member States for their collaboration, trust, and shared vision of regional unity. Their steadfast commitment to ASEAN's principles and practices has been the cornerstone of its progress. The dedication of the Member States to intra-regional cooperation, integration, and open regionalism has demonstrated how collective efforts can yield lasting peace, stability, and prosperity for Southeast Asia.

I also acknowledge the invaluable contributions of ASEAN's dialogue partners, development partners, business councils, think tanks and the Economic Research Institute of ASEAN and East Asia (ERIA). Their engagement, insights, and partnerships have greatly enhanced ASEAN's ability to address complex challenges and strengthen its global relevance. Their support reflects the spirit of inclusivity and shared responsibility that defines ASEAN's approach to regional and international collaboration.

Although my formal tenure at the ASEAN Secretariat ended in 2011, my commitment to ASEAN remains strong. I am deeply engaged in thinking, writing, and contributing to ASEAN's journey both as an academic and a practitioner. ASEAN's ideals and transformative potential continue to inspire me in my ongoing work. I believe that its vision for a unified, resilient, and prosperous Southeast Asia remains as critical today as ever. This book is not only a reflection of my experiences but also a testament to the collective efforts of everyone who has been part of ASEAN's remarkable journey.

To all who have walked this path with me, thank you for your dedication, vision, and belief in the power of regional unity.

Table of Contents

Introduction:

ASEAN
– A Pillar of Regional Stability & Multilateral Engagement

"At the time that the Foreign Ministers of the five states signed the Bangkok Declaration establishing ASEAN in 1967, regionalism and regional identity were new concepts that did not readily inspire public support. For we had long maintained strong political, economic, and cultural ties with others outside the region. We identified more with them than with ourselves of the region. But since then, there has emerged a new consciousness, and we have undergone fundamental and wilful changes ... The Association has given our respective countries the framework within which to strengthen social, economic, and cultural ties, and to develop cooperation where, hitherto, none had existed."

Thailand's Prime Minister Kukrit Pramoj at the opening of the Meeting of the Heads of Government in Bali, Indonesia on February 23, 1976

Southeast Asia is a region profoundly shaped by the collaborative spirit of its countries. They benefit from a relationship with the Association of Southeast Asian Nations, or simply ASEAN. Over the past five decades, ASEAN has strived to evolve into a central institution that contours Southeast Asia's political, economic, and security landscape, aiming to play a constructive role on the international stage. Imagine ASEAN as the hidden engine driving Southeast Asia's remarkable transformation, a tapestry woven from the diverse cultures, histories, and aspirations of over 680 million people. This book invites you to examine how ASEAN has become a cornerstone of regional stability, a catalyst for economic growth, and a platform for meaningful engagement with the world's major powers.

You may wonder why this book is an essential read. Consider the implications: ASEAN's policies and partnerships may not only affect the countries within the region but also determine how the world interacts with Southeast Asia. Whether you're a student eager to understand the intricacies of regional politics, a business professional exploring new markets, or simply someone captivated by regional and global affairs, this book is your gateway to comprehending the multifaceted mechanics of ASEAN. You will discover the organisation's significant achievements, challenges, and goals to play an indispensable role in today's interconnected world.

Why Transformative ASEAN?

The book title "transformative" ASEAN was deliberately chosen to encapsulate the essence of ASEAN's dynamic evolution in response to a rapidly changing world. The term "transformative" reflects the organisation's ongoing journey and proactive stance in navigating the complexities of regional and global challenges. ASEAN is not merely waiting for change to happen but actively seizing opportunities as they arise, recognising the need to embrace transformation and innovation to maintain its relevance. This is especially crucial in today's fast-paced environment, where geopolitical dynamics shift rapidly, and economic landscapes evolve. By adapting its strategies and frameworks, ASEAN has positioned itself to tackle emerging issues from economic integration and environmental sustainability to security threats and public health challenges.

Interestingly, ASEAN's relative weakness as a grouping compared to the major powers is actually its strength. This irony allows ASEAN to cultivate its unique identity, focusing on collaborative diplomacy rather than confrontation. As a result, its partners are less intimidated, promoting a conducive environment for dialogue and cooperation. ASEAN is seen as a convener of strategic meetings and plays a vital role in managing and diffusing tensions in Southeast Asia. Doing so enhances regional relevance by promoting unity among its member states while engaging meaningfully with external partners.

As the author who has had the privilege of working closely with ASEAN as a professional staff of the ASEAN Secretariat through participation in various ASEAN summits, ministers' meetings, and dialogue partners discussions over 15 years, I have witnessed firsthand the dynamics that shape this remarkable organisation. My experiences provide a unique lens through which to understand the formal processes of ASEAN and the informal interactions that often pave the way for collaboration, understanding, and decision-making among member states. Reflecting on my encounters with ASEAN leaders, ministers, and officials, I have come to appreciate the depth of commitment they bring to their roles. Their dedication to fostering unity and addressing common challenges is palpable, whether during intense negotiations or in casual dialogues in the corridors of power. These moments reveal the human element behind the policies and strategies, showcasing the shared aspirations and mutual respect underpinning ASEAN's ethos.

Through this book, I aim to share the narrative of ASEAN's journey and the rich anecdotes and insights from my experiences, illustrating the challenges and triumphs of ASEAN as it transforms itself to meet the demands of a changing world. I invite you to join me in exploring ASEAN's transformative journey—understanding its past, engaging with its present, and envisioning its future as a pillar of stability and a champion of collaboration in Southeast Asia and beyond.

Overview of book

This book provides a structured exploration of ASEAN's journey from its founding to its current regional and international significance. Each chapter covers critical aspects of ASEAN's evolution, beginning with its core principles and the dynamic forces that have moulded its path. It starts with the foundations of ASEAN. Chapter 1 takes you back to the origins of ASEAN, where the visionary foreign ministers from Indonesia, Malaysia, the Philippines, Singapore, and Thailand came together to form an organisation dedicated to regional cooperation. You will learn about their challenges and how they turned a shared vision into a reality. The essence of their commitment is captured in the Bangkok Declaration of 1967, marking the birth of ASEAN as a testament to their determination to promote peace and stability in a region rife with tensions.

Building on these principles, Chapter 2 shares the foundational documents that formalise ASEAN's operations. For instance, the Treaty of Amity and Cooperation (TAC) of 1976 is central to ASEAN's philosophy, which promotes non-interference and mutual respect among member states. This chapter emphasises the importance of these principles in fostering a cooperative environment, ensuring that ASEAN remains a unique diplomatic entity that prioritises dialogue over conflict. Understanding these core documents is crucial for appreciating how ASEAN maintains its integrity and unity in a complex geopolitical landscape. As we delve into ASEAN's collaborative nature, you will understand the significance of the "ASEAN Way". While some may criticise this approach for being slow or overly cautious, its focus on consensus-building, dialogue, and mutual respect has been vital for maintaining regional peace. Picture a community where nations once at odds are now working together to forge a shared future. This balancing act allows every member state—a democracy, monarchy, or one-party state—to engage in constructive dialogue.

In Chapter 3, we shift our attention to the significance of the ASEAN Charter, adopted in 2007, which formalised ASEAN's structure and operations. This vital document lays out the vision for an integrated ASEAN community, emphasising the importance of the three pillars: political security, economic, and socio-cultural. By establishing clear rules and regulations, the Charter enhances ASEAN's accountability and effectiveness, providing tools and a roadmap for member states to work together in addressing everyday challenges while promoting regional stability and prosperity.

Economics plays a significant role in this narrative. In this regard, Chapter 4 delves into the ASEAN Economic Community (AEC) and its pivotal role in driving regional economic integration. As one of the world's fastest-growing economic regions, ASEAN aims to create a single market and production base, enabling the free flow of goods, services, investment, and skilled labour. You'll learn about the challenges and opportunities of this integration and how initiatives like the ASEAN Free Trade Area (AFTA) have transformed the economic landscape, ultimately benefiting millions of people in the region.

The story doesn't end there. Security is another critical aspect of ASEAN's mission. In Chapter 5, we explore how ASEAN navigates the complexities of political and security cooperation. The ASEAN Political Security Community (APSC) aims to ensure regional peace and stability through dialogue and collaboration. You will discover how ASEAN addresses traditional security threats like territorial disputes, particularly in the South China Sea, while confronting non-traditional challenges such as terrorism, transnational crime, and climate change. ASEAN seeks to build a secure future for its member states by fostering an environment of trust and mutual respect.

We then shift gears to the social-cultural aspects of ASEAN cooperation, which are as important as its economic integration and political security cooperation. It is the glue for bringing the ASEAN nations together and creating an identity for the people to coalesce. In Chapter 6, we learn about the importance of the ASEAN Socio-Cultural Community (ASCC) and its functions, such as promoting people-to-people connectivity, cultural exchange, and social development initiatives that strengthen the bonds among member nations. You will discover more about various programs that aim to enhance citizens' quality of life, address social inequalities, and promote awareness of ASEAN identity. This commitment to social cohesion is essential for ensuring a harmonious and integrated regional community.

We move into the external dynamics of ASEAN's global engagement in Chapter 7, where we explore ASEAN's external relations and the vital role of its dialogue partners. This chapter illustrates how ASEAN engages with global and regional powers like the United States, China, Russia, India, Japan, and the European Union, fostering partnerships that extend beyond trade to encompass security and cultural exchange. You will see that ASEAN positions itself to become a key player on the Asia Pacific stage, balancing interests among its partners while striving to maintain its centrality in regional affairs.

From Chapters 8 to 11, we will explore the future trajectory of ASEAN, covering the economic, political security, climate change and sustainability, and external relations. We will also study the ASEAN centrality aspect and its strategic importance to the Association as it intensifies its community-building efforts and relations with its partners and plays a constructive regional role.

Chapter 8 examines trade and innovation trends within the region, highlighting how ASEAN adapts to globalisation and technological advancements. Through various initiatives to enhance competitiveness and foster sustainable growth, the chapter emphasises the vital role of innovation in driving economic progress and positioning ASEAN to thrive in a rapidly evolving global economy. Chapter 9 delves into ASEAN's comprehensive approach to security, addressing traditional threats like maritime disputes and non-traditional security challenges like cybersecurity.

As we transition to the chapters on sustainable development and global engagement, Chapter 10 emphasises ASEAN's dedication to promoting environmental stewardship and climate action. By showcasing initiatives for green growth and disaster resilience, the chapter highlights ASEAN's commitment to balancing economic development with sustainability in the face of environmental challenges. Chapter 11 focuses on ASEAN's expanding role in international affairs, illustrating how the organisation steers complex diplomacy and strengthens partnerships with the major powers—this proactive approach positions ASEAN to become a constructive player in global governance. Chapter 12 discusses the concept of ASEAN centrality, emphasising the organisation's strategies to maintain relevance in a multipolar world while advocating for peace and stability in Southeast Asia. Collectively, these chapters provide a comprehensive overview of ASEAN's transformative journey and a potentially critical role in shaping the region's future and beyond.

Chapter 13 reflects the most significant lessons from ASEAN's development over the past five decades. It examines the critical elements contributing to its success, including consensus-based decision-making, the delicate balance between sovereignty and regional cooperation, and its ability to adapt to geopolitical and economic challenges. The chapter distils ten key learnings that highlight ASEAN's resilience, diplomacy, and evolving role in regional and global contexts, providing a roadmap for the future of Southeast Asia's regional cooperation.

Lastly, in bonus Chapter 14, we look at the impressive statistics that underscore the significance of ASEAN in the global landscape. This chapter presents a compelling data collection highlighting ASEAN's demographic diversity, dividend, economic achievements, and regional influence. From population figures and trade statistics to insights on sustainable development and social progress, these facts illustrate how ASEAN has transformed into a vital economic powerhouse with a collective voice on the world stage. By showcasing the tangible impact of ASEAN's initiatives and the benefits experienced by its member states, the chapter serves as a powerful testament to the organisation's success and its ongoing journey towards greater integration and cooperation in Southeast Asia and globally.

In short, this book explores ASEAN's past and present while providing a trajectory for its future. Fuelled by the pressing need to remain relevant, ASEAN is driven to embrace transformation and seize every opportunity, reinforcing its leadership role in Southeast Asia—this commitment to adaptability and innovation positions ASEAN to become a dynamic force in an ever-evolving global landscape.

On this exploration, remember that ASEAN is more than a political entity; it symbolises hope, unity, and collaboration in a diverse and complex region. It embodies Southeast Asia's potential to carve out its own destiny on the international stage. Through insightful analysis, engaging anecdotes, and a deep dive into the mechanics of regional cooperation, you will uncover ASEAN's transformative journey and its significance in today's world.

By the time you reach the final pages of this book, you will have gained a comprehensive understanding of ASEAN's journey from its founding ideals to its current role in shaping Southeast Asia's destiny. In the process, you will uncover the stories, strategies, and aspirations defining ASEAN's transition and critical importance in shaping the region's dynamics. This book is designed not merely to inform you; it will equip you with the analytical tools necessary to critically engage with ASEAN's policies, strategies, and ongoing transformation.

> *"ASEAN has evolved from a modest organisation with five founding members into a crucial pillar of stability in Southeast Asia. Its ability to diffuse tensions, prevent conflicts, and foster regional unity is unparalleled in the history of regional organisations."*
>
> **Pushpanathan Sundram, Author**

Chapter 1

The Founding of ASEAN – From Idea to Reality

"What we have decided today is only a small beginning of what we hope will be a long and continuous sequence of accomplishments of which we ourselves, those who will join us later and the generations to come, can be proud. Let it be for Southeast Asia, a potentially rich region, rich in history, in spiritual as well as material resources and indeed for the whole ancient continent of Asia, the light of happiness and well-being that will shine over the uncounted millions of our struggling peoples."

Thailand's Foreign Minister Thanat Khoman at the signing of thc Bangkok Declaration, Bangkok, Thailand, August 8, 1967

Picture Southeast Asia in the 1960s, a region emerging from the shadows of colonialism, with newly independent nations striving to build their futures amidst a landscape of political unrest, historical mistrust, ideological divides, and superpower tensions. It was a time when Southeast Asian countries grappled with their newfound sovereignty and the external pressures of the Cold War, demanding alignment with either the United States or the Soviet Union. The urgent question of that era was, "How do we build a peaceful and stable future together?" This is where the story of ASEAN begins.

ASEAN's formation wasn't just a matter of political pragmatism but an act of vision. Leaders across the region understood that cooperation and not conflict would need to be the way forward for Southeast Asia to thrive. This chapter takes you on a journey from the turbulent 1960s, marked by strife and uncertainty, to the signing of the Bangkok Declaration in 1967 and beyond. You will discover the challenges, hopes, and aspirations of ASEAN's founding fathers, the complex dynamics that contributed to its formation, and the principles that would become the bedrock of Southeast Asia's regional architecture.

Southeast Asia in the 1960s

Let's start by understanding the context in which ASEAN emerged. The 1960s were tumultuous for Southeast Asia. Newly independent nations were not only dealing with self-governance challenges but also navigating a region divided by ideologies. While some countries leaned toward communism, others embraced capitalist economic models. The Cold War rivalry between the United States and the Soviet Union cast a long shadow over the region, with each superpower keen on extending its influence.

Southeast Asia was rife with internal tensions. Indonesia, Malaysia and the Philippines faced internal political challenges, civil unrest, and insurgencies. Indonesia's confrontation with Malaysia, famously known as *Konfrontasi,* had only recently ended, leaving wounds that would take time to heal. Southeast Asia was not naturally inclined toward unity. Instead, suspicion and historical rivalries marked the region. Yet, fortunately, the seeds of regional cooperation began to sprout in this atmosphere when these Southeast Asian countries found a common goal: the desire for stability, peace, and development amongst newly independent states. It became increasingly clear that these objectives could not be achieved in isolation. The idea of ASEAN was born from this realisation, a belief that regional challenges could be better faced together.

Early regional unity attempts

Before ASEAN emerged as a cornerstone of Southeast Asian cooperation, the region was a hotbed of ambitious but ultimately fragile alliances, each shaped by political turbulence, ideological divides, and clashing national interests of their time. In the wake of decolonisation and the Cold War's shadow, Southeast Asia was grappling with a mix of newfound independence and the looming threat of communism, prompting countries to seek regional unity. Yet the early attempts to create a unified grouping were riddled with setbacks, proving that the path to regional cooperation was anything but straightforward.

One of the earliest attempts was the Southeast Asia Treaty Organisation (SEATO), formed in 1954. Modelled after NATO, SEATO was designed as a bulwark against the spread of communism in Asia, bringing together countries like the United States, United Kingdom, Australia, and Pakistan alongside Southeast Asian nations like Thailand and the Philippines. However, SEATO's efforts to create a cohesive security alliance failed to resonate with the local political climate as most Southeast Asian countries saw it as an extension of Western influence rather than a regional effort. With members holding divergent political priorities and lacking a unified military structure, SEATO struggled to act decisively and dissolved quietly in 1977, ultimately failing to build the regional solidarity it envisioned.

Following SEATO's struggles, the Association of Southeast Asia (ASA) was established in 1961 by Malaysia, the Philippines, and Thailand. The formation of ASA marked a locally driven attempt at collaboration, focusing on economic, cultural, and technical cooperation among Southeast Asian nations. However, ASA quickly ran into roadblocks, primarily due to Malaysia's idea to create the Federation of Malaysia and the territorial dispute between Malaysia and the Philippines over the state of Sabah, which became a flashpoint of conflict. The tensions surrounding this dispute and other unresolved regional issues led to the ASA's rapid decline, revealing the fragile nature of the cooperation among these nations.

Not deterred by these setbacks, another attempt at regional unity was made in 1963 with the formation of MAPHILINDO, a proposed confederation of Malaya, the Philippines, and Indonesia. MAPHILINDO aimed to form a pan-Malay cultural and political entity, promoting regional solidarity and addressing shared interests. However, this organisation was born into a storm of ideological differences and unresolved tensions, particularly the *Konfrontasi* launched by Indonesia against the formation of the Federation of Malaysia, which it saw as a colonial plot. Within a month, MAPHILINDO collapsed under the weight of these disputes, ideological clashes, and its lack of a concrete institutional framework, fading as quickly as it had formed.

These early attempts showed the region's yearning for unity but exposed the deep-rooted complexities of Southeast Asian politics: territorial disputes, ideological rifts, and post-colonial nationalisms that refused to be swept under the rug. Each failure, however, was a lesson in the need for a more inclusive, pragmatic, and resilient regional framework, leading to the formation of ASEAN in 1967.

ASEAN's founding

The founders of ASEAN were not just political figures of their time; they were architects of a new Southeast Asian identity, weaving a regional fabric out of nations that had often been embroiled in disputes and conflicts. Each founder brought a unique perspective and motivation to contour the organisation's direction, laying the foundation for a more united and resilient Southeast Asia. These leaders—Adam Malik of Indonesia, Tun Abdul Razak of Malaysia, Narciso Ramos of the Philippines, S. Rajaratnam of Singapore, and Thanat Khoman of Thailand are the pioneers who crafted the vision and mission that would transform the region's future.

Adam Malik, the Foreign Minister of Indonesia, played a crucial role in fostering diplomacy and cooperation in a region still reeling from political upheaval. With its strategic position and vast population, Indonesia was a dominant force in Southeast Asia. However, Indonesia's regional relationships suffered during the turbulent period of *Konfrontasi,* a conflict with Malaysia in the early 1960s over territorial and ideological disputes. Adam Malik saw ASEAN as an opportunity to repair Indonesia's strained relations and promote peace. He firmly believed in using diplomacy to resolve conflicts and strengthen ties among neighbouring countries. Under his leadership, Indonesia transitioned from a confrontational stance to cooperation, marking a shift from regional dominance to partnership. His vision was for Indonesia to emerge not as a regional antagonist but as a key player in a broader Southeast Asian community, working together for peace and development.

Tun Abdul Razak, Malaysia's Deputy Prime Minister and Foreign Minister, was another mainspring behind

ASEAN's creation. Razak was a pragmatist who believed in the power of regional unity as a counterbalance to the growing threat of communism, which was spreading across Southeast Asia during the Cold War era. For Razak, ASEAN was more than just a diplomatic entity; it was a means to strengthen collective security and ensure that Southeast Asia did not become a battleground for external ideological conflicts. He understood that fostering economic development and social progress was integral to securing political stability and preventing the spread of communism within and across the borders of member states. He substantially steered Malaysia from suspicion and animosity, particularly toward Indonesia after *Konfrontasi,* to a cooperative and collaborative relationship. This shift in Malaysia's foreign policy was significant in building trust within the newly formed ASEAN.

Narciso Ramos, the Philippines' Foreign Secretary, was deeply committed to using economic cooperation as a tool for peacebuilding and development. He recognised Southeast Asia's long-term stability depended on political agreements and economic collaboration that would lead to shared prosperity. Ramos was a seasoned diplomat, having served as a journalist, lawyer, assemblyman, and ambassador before entering politics. His wealth of experience in international relations equipped him with the foresight to see ASEAN as a platform for advancing political stability and economic growth. He envisioned a region where trade, investment, and development initiatives would lift the standard of living for all member states and create interdependent economies that would deter conflicts. Ramos was instrumental in advocating for the economic provisions in the Bangkok Declaration, ensuring that ASEAN's objectives went beyond security concerns and laid the groundwork for future economic cooperation.

S. Rajaratnam, Singapore's first Foreign Minister, brought a unique perspective as the representative of a small, newly independent city-state with a diverse population and a strategic location. For Rajaratnam, ASEAN's creation was vital for Singapore's survival amidst a turbulent regional environment. His focus was on ensuring stability and fostering a sense of regional identity. Rajaratnam strongly advocated for ASEAN's principle of non-interference, emphasising the importance of mutual respect and sovereignty among member states. He believed regional unity could only be achieved if countries refrained from meddling in each other's internal affairs. At the same time, he advocated for building a sense of "ASEAN-ness" among member states, promoting cultural ties, understanding, and a shared vision for the region's future. Rajaratnam's diplomatic skills were critical in bridging the cultural and political divides among the founding nations; his vision of a harmonious and interlinked Southeast Asia still resonates in ASEAN's ethos today.

Thanat Khoman, Thailand's Foreign Minister, played a key role in the conception and realisation of ASEAN.

Often referred to as one of the primary architects of ASEAN, Thanat was a seasoned diplomat who recognised the strategic need for regional cooperation in a time of growing communist influence. Thailand shared borders with countries experiencing intense communist insurgencies, and Thanat believed that ASEAN could serve as a collective defence against this rising threat. His vision was for ASEAN to provide a platform for regional stability, not just as a diplomatic tool but as a collective security framework. He was known for his pragmatic approach, advocating for practical and action-oriented regional cooperation that could yield tangible peace and economic development benefits.

Thanat's personal diplomacy was crucial in bringing the initial five members together to sign the Bangkok Declaration in Thailand. He skilfully managed differing priorities and persuaded his counterparts to see the long-term benefits of cooperation. Thanat's insight into the importance of regional autonomy was also significant. He advocated for a Southeast Asia free from external domination, be it from colonial powers or Cold War superpowers. His contributions were instrumental in setting the tone for ASEAN's policy of neutrality and independence, ensuring that Southeast Asian nations themselves would decide the region's future.

Each founder brought a distinct vision and set of priorities to the creation of ASEAN in 1967. As stated in the Bangkok Declaration, the principal objective of ASEAN is to accelerate economic growth, social progress and cultural development in the region through joint endeavours in the spirit of equality and partnership. The Declaration also stated that ASEAN would strive to maintain close and beneficial cooperation with existing international and regional organisations, promote regional peace and stability through the rule of law, and provide assistance to each other in the form of training and research facilities in the educational, professional, technical and administrative spheres. These leaders understood the challenges of their time and foresaw the opportunities that regional cooperation could bring. The creation of ASEAN was a testament to their ability to look beyond immediate political differences and envision a future of shared prosperity, security, and cultural ties. Through their leadership, ASEAN was founded as a grouping committed to mutual respect, non-interference, and shared progress.

Their legacy is seen today in how ASEAN has grown from a small five-member organisation to a ten-member regional body. The principles and vision laid out by these founders have allowed ASEAN to navigate decades of challenges and maintain its relevance and influence on the international scene. Their leadership continues to inspire ASEAN's ongoing journey to deeper integration and collective resilience as Southeast Asia becomes an increasingly dynamic and interconnected region globally.

Naming ASEAN

The name "ASEAN" was coined during the historic Bangkok discussions in 1967 among the founding fathers of ASEAN. The original designation, "Association of Southeast Asia," lacked a suitable sounding acronym. Recognising this, Thanat asked Adam Malik, his Indonesian counterpart, since the country is known for creating acronyms. The latter suggested inserting the word "Nations," transforming the name to "Association of Southeast Asian Nations," and pronouncing the acronym "AH-SEE-AN," marking the first utterance of "ASEAN."

This deliberate naming choice signified a departure from earlier regional initiatives like SEATO, ASA, and MAPHILINDO, which had either failed due to internal conflicts or lacked comprehensive regional representation. By including "Nations," it emphasised the sovereignty and equality of each member state in a diverse region with post-colonial sensitivities.

The term "Nations" indicated an openness to future expansion, envisioning an organisation that would eventually encompass all Southeast Asian countries. This vision materialised over the years, with ASEAN expanding to include Brunei, Vietnam, Laos, Myanmar, and Cambodia, representing the entire region.

Weaving together a vision

Amidst the geopolitical complexities of the time, the formation of ASEAN arose from a pressing need for dialogue and unity among nations that had previously experienced political tensions and conflicts. As these leaders convened, they recognised that the fragmented economies and the divergent political objectives of Southeast Asian countries hindered the region's potential for growth. During discussions leading to the formation of ASEAN, Thanat reflected on the urgency for cooperation, stating that at the banquet marking the reconciliation between the three disputants (Indonesia, Malaysia, and the Philippines), he broached the idea of forming another organisation for regional cooperation.

The informal negotiations that followed were characterised by what the ministers called "sports-shirt diplomacy". This relaxed atmosphere allowed for open discussions, fostering goodwill and camaraderie as the leaders navigated their differences. During the rounds of discussions and deliberations, they crafted a brief yet powerful document: the ASEAN Declaration. This non-binding declaration outlined the aims and purposes of the newly formed association, emphasising cooperation in economic, social, cultural, and technical fields alongside a commitment to promoting regional peace and stability through respect for justice and adherence to the principles of the United Nations Charter.

As the foreign ministers signed the ASEAN Declaration on August 8, 1967, they articulated a shared vision: a region united by friendship and cooperation, striving to overcome the historical and political divides that had characterised Southeast Asia. Narciso R. Ramos of the

Philippines poignantly remarked on the significance of this collective effort, stating that the fragmented economies of Southeast Asia carried the seeds of weakness in their incapacity for growth and ASEAN, therefore, could marshal the still untapped potentials of the rich region through more substantial united action. His words captured the essence of ASEAN's founding: the recognition that member states could leverage their strengths through collaboration for mutual benefit.

Continuation of sports shirt diplomacy

Thanks to the founding fathers, the tradition of sports shirt diplomacy continues today. I fondly recall moments when heads of government and foreign ministers would huddle together, whether in meeting rooms or on a golf course, to address pressing issues. In these informal settings, some of ASEAN's most challenging matters were tackled—ranging from tensions between member states to the ratification of the ASEAN Charter—all while striving to uphold ASEAN's reputation within the international community.

One incident stands out vividly in my memory. It was in 2007 in New York during an informal meeting with the ASEAN foreign ministers. What began as an informal gathering quickly transformed into a critical drafting session. The gathering coincided with the UN General Assembly meeting, where ASEAN foreign ministers meet regularly to exchange views and coordinate positions on developments in ASEAN and the UN. It was also the time the Saffron Revolution in Myanmar was escalating with violence and suppression.

On September 27, protests surged in Yangon, and tragically, a Japanese reporter, Kenji Nagai, was killed amidst the chaos. Soldiers fired tear gas at crowds of 10,000, and global outrage grew louder as the military crackdown continued. By the next day, Myanmar's military junta had cut off internet access, and troops fired bullets at crowds. They used force to disperse protesters, and soldiers raided monasteries in their efforts to quash the uprising. Amidst all this, a junta general called on senior monks to rein in the protests, intensifying the pressure.

The European Union considered further sanctions, the United Nations named a special envoy, and China and Japan agreed to cooperate in addressing the situation. Meanwhile, Japan was demanding a full account of the journalist's death. The urgency in the room was palpable. As ministers sat down to discuss, there was a pressing need to craft ASEAN's response that would balance the region's principles of peace, dialogue, and non-interference while addressing the harsh reality of the unfolding crisis.

Against this backdrop, the gathering turned into an ad hoc drafting session. In a rare and unprecedented move, ASEAN openly condemned the actions of Myanmar's military. A poignant ASEAN Chair statement outlining ASEAN's stance and concerns over the events in Myanmar was quickly composed with the assistance of the ASEAN Secretariat, which I was a part of. The statement issued on September 28 strongly condemned reports of violence against demonstrators. It urged Myanmar's government to cease violence, exercise restraint, pursue political solutions, and work toward peaceful democratic transition and national reconciliation. The statement also voiced concern over the impact of Myanmar's actions on ASEAN's credibility.

Thus, an informal gathering transformed into a pivotal moment for ASEAN, as participants addressed an escalating key issue, built consensus, and conducted impactful diplomacy. These moments were more than just decision-making processes. They were opportunities to build relationships, understand each nation's unique stance, and reach consensus through mutual respect and trust. The ability of ASEAN leaders and ministers to engage in such informal diplomacy underscored their commitment to fostering peace and stability in the region. It proved that sometimes, crucial decisions are best made away from formal meeting rooms over a meal or a round of golf, with candid conversation and open minds.

Non-interference and consensus

ASEAN's core principles of non-interference and consensus form the bedrock of its diplomacy and decision-making, shaping how the organisation interacts internally and traverses the wider geopolitical landscape. These principles, embraced since its founding, have allowed

ASEAN to develop a unique approach to regional cooperation, one that values harmony and unity but often grapples with the complexities of balancing respect for sovereignty with the need for decisive action.

For a moment, envision a room filled with representatives from ten diverse countries, each bringing their historical baggage, political systems, and national interests. The principle of non-interference acts like an unspoken rule in that room, encouraging respect and diplomacy. Essentially, it's about giving member states the space to govern their affairs without pressure from external judgment. Given the backdrop of newly independent nations with fresh memories of colonialism, it made perfect sense. Non-interference was a pact to build mutual trust and focus on common goals rather than getting entangled in the complex internal affairs of neighbours.

This hands-off approach did, and still does, serve a crucial purpose. It offers a buffer that prevents conflicts from escalating within the ASEAN family and allows cooperation without fear of condemnation or external meddling. The principle helped ASEAN build confidence among its members during the formative years, a period when many of these states were still healing from their own internal strife or regional conflicts. But this policy is not without its pitfalls. By prioritising sovereignty over intervention, ASEAN often finds itself limited in its ability to address human rights abuses, political turmoil, or social injustices happening within its member states.

Take Myanmar, for example, where internal conflict and allegations of human rights violations have placed the country under international scrutiny. The principle of non-interference restricts ASEAN's ability to take decisive action, leading to criticism that the organisation sometimes acts too cautiously when addressing pressing issues within its own borders.

This brings us to the principle of consensus-based decision-making, colloquially known as the "ASEAN Way." Unlike many international and regional organisations that rely on majority votes to make decisions, ASEAN operates on the norms of *Musyawarah* (consultation) and *Musfakat* (consensus). It is more of a conflict avoidance than a problem-solving approach mechanism, relying on informal negotiations to manage disputes. This approach affirms sovereignty and non-interference, helping to maintain harmonious intra-ASEAN relations while preserving bilateral ties.

Every member has an equal say, and unanimity is required before any major policy or action is agreed upon. At its best, this consensus model is an exercise in diplomacy, encouraging dialogue and ensuring that each member state feels heard and valued. There's no "winner takes all" mentality here, only a collective drive to reach a mutual understanding. However, the downside to this approach is apparent.

Consensus often results in protracted discussions and compromises. When the issues are contentious, the process can slow to a crawl. A single dissenting voice can delay or even derail decisions affecting the region. In practice, this can mean that ASEAN's policies, while well-intentioned, may be diluted or limited in scope simply because every member must agree. When confronted with complex and divisive issues, such as territorial disputes in the South China Sea or disagreements over handling political crises, the consensus model has sometimes struggled to produce timely and effective responses.

It's worth noting, however, that this consensus approach stems from a broader cultural value that pervades the region: the preference for harmony and avoiding open confrontation. It reflects the desire to build a sense of community and maintain unity, so ASEAN has been cautious about imposing decisions that might antagonise or alienate any member. In a way, the ASEAN Way has been a diplomatic masterstroke, ensuring that decisions are inclusive, smaller countries have a voice alongside larger countries in the regional grouping, and differences are resolved through quiet negotiation rather than public discord.

Similarly, the principle of non-interference has been instrumental in creating a stable and cooperative environment, but it also presents challenges. The balance between upholding sovereignty and advocating for collective action is delicate. The principle of non-interference often means ASEAN treads carefully on sensitive issues, avoiding hard stances that might be seen as infringing on a member's sovereignty. Therefore, the principles of consensus and non-interference that have made ASEAN what it is today are also the same ones that occasionally limit its ability to become a swift and decisive regional leader.

As ASEAN continues to evolve, the principles of non-interference and consensus will undoubtedly be tested by new challenges—whether they address human rights concerns, manage territorial disputes, or respond to global crises. How ASEAN adapts these principles to modern realities will determine its ability to uphold its mission as a cohesive, responsive, and resilient regional organisation. While the ASEAN Way may sometimes be imperfect, it has nonetheless carved out a distinct path for the organisation, one that prioritises unity and cooperation in an often-fractious world.

Building trust and cooperation

Visualise the early days of ASEAN as a balancing act, a cautious, measured waltz between neighbours who were only beginning to understand one another. Every step was tentative, testing the waters of cooperation, unsure of how to move forward without stepping on each other's toes. Building trust was the foundation of it all. In a region marked by a history of conflicts, misunderstandings and power struggles, the idea of sitting together at the same table was a brave new concept.

These formative years weren’t about grand declarations or sweeping policies; they were about dialogue. The real success of ASEAN in its infancy was creating a space where conversations could happen, and countries could see each other as partners and not rivals. A major milestone on the path to trust was the signing of the Zone of Peace, Freedom, and Neutrality Declaration (ZOPFAN) in 1971. It was a bold step and a shared commitment that Southeast Asia would remain a region free from external interference, standing united against being dragged into the intense proxy battles of the Cold War.

In these early days of ASEAN, meetings were far from the structured, heavily scheduled affairs we see today. Discussions unfolded in a more relaxed atmosphere, almost like family gatherings where leaders could speak freely. Decisions were often made over a casual cup of coffee, durian-eating sessions, or even while playing a round of golf. This laid-back approach was intentional; it fostered genuine conversation, eased tensions, and allowed the leaders to examine sensitive topics without the pressure of formal negotiations or the watchful eyes of their ministers and officials.

Indeed, during these simple, unpretentious conversations, the seeds of trust were sown. Leaders began to understand one another, see beyond borders and politics, and focus on what could be achieved together. This emerging bond would prove vital, creating the foundations for deeper collaboration and more ambitious goals in the years that followed.

Expanding the ASEAN family

The growth of ASEAN was like welcoming new members to an ever-expanding family, each bringing its own flavour, history, and experiences to the table. Starting as a modest group of five, the organisation gradually opened its doors to more Southeast Asian countries, fostering a sense of regional unity that was far more ambitious than its founders could have initially imagined.

In 1984, Brunei became the sixth member, shortly after gaining independence. It was a significant addition—a small but wealthy nation that would contribute to ASEAN's political and economic diversity. Then came the 1990s, a decade of rapid expansion that saw ASEAN transform into an inclusive regional organisation in Southeast Asia. In 1995, Vietnam joined the fold, a momentous step that symbolised bridging past ideological divides after decades of conflict. Vietnam's entry marked a turning point in regional relations, moving beyond Cold War rivalries to embrace cooperation and integration.

Two years later, in 1997, Laos and Myanmar joined ASEAN. The inclusion of these countries posed its own set of challenges and opportunities. Laos brought a landlocked perspective, highlighting the need for greater regional connectivity. Myanmar's membership was more controversial, bringing global attention to issues of governance, human rights, and political reforms within ASEAN's framework. Yet the decision to include Myanmar also demonstrated ASEAN's approach to engagement over isolation, seeking to encourage gradual progress from within the organisation.

I remember an intense meeting among the ASEAN foreign ministers back in 1997, where the discussion centred on a highly contentious issue: Should Myanmar be admitted into ASEAN, or should we delay its entry? ASEAN felt the weight of pressure from the European Union and the United States, both questioning the Association's approach to regional membership. The decision to admit Myanmar was not just a matter of regional politics; it represented a critical moment that significantly strained ASEAN's relations with its dialogue partners in the West.

The European Union and the United States strongly urged that Myanmar be excluded from ASEAN, pointing to its poor record on democracy and human rights. Despite this external pressure, ASEAN ultimately decided to proceed with Myanmar's admission. The rationale was multifaceted: for one, ASEAN, founded in 1967 to limit outside influence in Southeast Asia, was unwilling to let Western powers dictate its membership policy, especially based on internal political practices. Furthermore, there was the lingering apprehension that excluding Myanmar could push it further into China's sphere of influence, impacting regional stability.

ASEAN foreign ministers shared an interesting perspective on Myanmar's admission into ASEAN with a few of us present. They used the relationship as a metaphor for marriage and courtship; they believed in formalising the relationship first and engaging in courtship afterwards. This perspective implies that admitting Myanmar into ASEAN would create a platform for dialogue and engagement, allowing for gradual improvements in governance and human rights over time. ASEAN's stance reflected a belief that inclusion could nurture a cooperative spirit and facilitate deeper regional integration.

While ASEAN's admission of Myanmar aimed to carry out dialogue and regional stability, the outcome has fallen short of these intentions. Myanmar's continued human rights abuses and lack of democratic governance have strained ASEAN's image, particularly following the military coup in February 2021, which led to widespread violence and repression. The Association's response, captured in the "Five-Point Consensus," has been criticised for its lack of enforcement and tangible impact, as ASEAN refrained from taking a firmer stance against the military regime. This has impacted ASEAN's image as a promoter of peace, stability, and human rights to some extent. The ongoing conflict in Myanmar not only destabilises the nation but also poses challenges to the cohesion of the ASEAN Community, highlighting the complexities of balancing regional diplomacy with the promotion of democratic norms and human rights among its member states.

The final piece of the puzzle fell into place in 1999, with Cambodia becoming the tenth member of ASEAN, after a delay of two years stemming from a power struggle between the two major political parties, the Cambodian People's Party (CPP) and the royalist Funcinpec Party, which led to instability in the country. ASEAN was concerned that admitting Cambodia in 1997 amidst such turmoil could undermine its commitment to political stability and mutual respect among member states. It wasn't until the political situation stabilised and a more cooperative government was established that Cambodia was finally welcomed into the organisation in 1999, marking the complete geographical representation of mainland and maritime Southeast Asia. Each new member added to the complexity of ASEAN, bringing different governance systems, economic conditions, and social challenges. However, this diversity also enriched the organisation, creating a platform for collaboration across a broad spectrum of regional interests.

Today, ASEAN's family is poised to grow even further, with Timor-Leste on the path to potentially becoming its 11th member. Already the 166th member of the World Trade Organisation (WTO) in August 2024, Timor-Leste's inclusion in ASEAN would reflect the organisation's commitment to inclusivity and regional integration. The country is the 11th Least Developed Country (LDC) to accede to the WTO since the organisation was established in 1995.

At the 42nd ASEAN Summit in May 2023, ASEAN leaders adopted an objective and criteria-based Roadmap for Timor-Leste's full membership, marking a significant step forward in the region's commitment to inclusivity and integration. The country's progress will be closely monitored, with regular updates provided to the ASEAN

Coordinating Council (ACC) to ensure the full and effective fulfilment of the Roadmap's criteria.

This development highlights ASEAN's role as a community that values diversity, unity, and regional collaboration. ASEAN Member States and external partners have been called upon to extend capacity-building assistance and other necessary support to help Timor-Leste meet the criteria outlined in the Roadmap. The country's inclusion in ASEAN will further underscore the organisation's dedication to fostering peace, stability, and sustainable development across Southeast Asia.

Challenges in ASEAN's early decades

The early years of ASEAN were like navigating a ship through stormy seas. Progress was often slow, and the organisation constantly battled economic, political, and external challenges to steer a steady course. While ASEAN's vision of unity and cooperation was bold, the path to achieving it was far from straightforward.

One of the toughest hurdles was the economic divide among member states. Visualise Singapore progressing ahead economically, while just across the water, countries like Indonesia and the Philippines faced deep developmental struggles and poverty. The economic disparities were glaring, creating friction whenever regional economic policies were discussed. Every decision required ensuring that all member nations, wealthy and developing, felt heard and supported, a tricky task that sometimes slowed progress. It wasn't just about creating unity; it was about ensuring unity worked for everyone, regardless of their economic starting point.

Then, there were the pressures of the Cold War, like dark clouds hanging over ASEAN's ambitions. The organisation's neutral stance was clear: Southeast Asia would not be a playing field for the superpowers. However, holding firm in the middle of a global standoff between the United States and the Soviet Union was easier said than done. The tension was intense, and ASEAN members had to tread carefully in their individual relationships with these superpowers. The non-alignment was a shield, but it didn't always protect the organisation from the relentless geopolitical pressures of the time.

ASEAN had its fair share of internal storms. Political disputes and governance challenges within member countries were part of the region's reality. Here was another challenge: ASEAN's guiding principle of non-interference. While it showed respect for each member's sovereignty, it also meant that ASEAN often stood on the sidelines of pressing political issues. This approach limits the organisation's ability to effectively address conflicts or human rights issues within its borders. Yet, despite these limitations, the grouping found its way. ASEAN members prioritised shared goals and dialogue, building bridges rather than walls and placing cooperation over confrontation.

The story of ASEAN is one of hope, resilience, and a vision that has stood the test of time. What started as a modest initiative in 1967 has blossomed into a dynamic organisation that fosters regional cooperation and contributes to global discourse. The founding principles laid out in the Bangkok Declaration and the Treaty of Amity and Cooperation (TAC) were the building blocks of an enduring legacy that still guides ASEAN today. ASEAN's reach extends far beyond Southeast Asia. It has evolved into a powerful example of how nations, despite their differences, can unite under a shared purpose and vision for peace, stability, and progress. The principles of consensus and non-interference, initially seen as cautious diplomacy, have proven to be the glue that holds a diverse region together, allowing for dialogue and collaboration even in times of disagreement.

As you continue reading, you will uncover how ASEAN's journey has been one of growth and transformation. From navigating the challenges of its early years to becoming a major regional actor, ASEAN's evolution tells a story of adaptability, strength, and unity amidst shifting politics, economic changes, and security challenges. It is a legacy still in the making that continues to inspire and direct the future of Southeast Asia.

> *"The ASEAN way, grounded in consensus and non-interference, has provided the region with a unique approach to maintaining peace, which has helped avert large-scale conflict for more than five decades."*
>
> **Pushpanathan Sundram, Author**

Chapter 2

ASEAN's Core Documents & Principles

"We have just put our signatures on very important documents [Declaration of ASEAN Concord and Treaty of Amity and Cooperation in Southeast Asia] ...They are the manifestation of our determination to promote peace, progress, stability and welfare of our peoples through closer cooperation in all aspects."

Indonesia's President Suharto at the Closing of the Meeting of the Heads of Government, Bali, Indonesia, February 24, 1976

ASEAN's story is one of evolution and growth, guided by foundational documents that serve as the legal and strategic bedrock of the organisation. Since its inception in 1967, ASEAN has relied on a series of agreements and declarations that have moulded its development from a small regional forum into one of the most influential organisations. From the Bangkok Declaration to the ASEAN Charter, these documents outline principles and practices that continue to guide ASEAN's journey. In this chapter, we explore the milestones that defined ASEAN's growth, understanding briefly how each document contributed to its vision, principles, and role.

1967: Bangkok Declaration

The story begins on August 8, 1967, when the five Southeast Asian nations came together in Bangkok to sign the Bangkok Declaration, which would give birth to ASEAN. This meeting was a bold step toward a shared regional identity, one that sought to transcend the colonial legacies, conflicts, and geopolitical tensions of the Cold War era. As this founding document became known, the Bangkok Declaration called for unity and cooperation among the member states.

The declaration laid out ambitious objectives to accelerate economic growth, social progress, and cultural development across the region. The signatories believed building economic cooperation would be key to collective stability and prosperity. Peace and stability were at the heart of this declaration, which sought to create an environment where Southeast Asian countries could live in harmony, unaffected by external interference and ideological conflicts.

Equally important was the provision to respect each member state's sovereignty and avoid meddling in each other's domestic affairs. This approach was necessary for countries with diverse political systems and histories of conflict and mistrust. It laid the foundation for a consensus-driven ASEAN, where dialogue and collaboration became the preferred methods for resolving disputes and setting policies. The Bangkok Declaration was not a detailed blueprint but a statement of intent, setting the tone for a future of cooperation, peace, and shared growth.

1976: ASEAN Concord I

Almost ten years after its founding, ASEAN took a decisive step towards deepening regional cooperation with the signing of the Declaration of ASEAN Concord I during the 1st ASEAN Summit in Bali, Indonesia, in 1976. This landmark document, also referred to as Bali Concord I, provided ASEAN with its first structured framework for collaboration across political, economic, social, and cultural dimensions. By this time, ASEAN had matured as an organisation, and its leaders recognised the need for a clearer, more formalised approach to navigate the region's growing challenges and opportunities amidst Cold War tensions and rapid economic shifts.

The Concord set a bold political vision for the region, emphasising the shared responsibility of maintaining peace and stability. It reinforced ASEAN's commitment to resolving disputes peacefully, echoing principles formalised in the Treaty of Amity and Cooperation (TAC), signed at the same summit. It also supported the establishment of the Zone of Peace, Freedom, and Neutrality (ZOPFAN), underscoring ASEAN's determination to shield Southeast Asia from the influence of external powers. Furthermore, it called for strengthening ASEAN's institutional mechanisms, including the formal establishment of the ASEAN Secretariat, to enhance its ability to respond to regional issues collectively.

Economically, the Concord prioritised cooperation to promote shared prosperity and reduce development gaps among member states. It proposed the establishment of joint economic ventures, particularly in critical sectors such as trade, agriculture, and industrial development. These initiatives aimed to address regional challenges by encouraging collaborative approaches to resource management. While ambitious, these proposals laid the groundwork for later milestones in economic integration, such as the ASEAN Free Trade Area (AFTA) in the 1990s.

On social and cultural fronts, the Concord embraced ASEAN's diversity as a strength. It advocated for regional collaboration in education, science, and cultural exchange to foster greater understanding and solidarity among ASEAN's peoples. It also highlighted the need to address pressing social issues, including rural development, population growth, and drug abuse, while promoting youth and women's participation in development efforts. The Concord reflected ASEAN's commitment to building a people-centred community by improving quality of life.

The ASEAN Concord I was a forward-thinking declaration of intent that laid the foundation for ASEAN's future integration efforts. While not legally binding, it served as a blueprint for regional collaboration and an articulation of the organisation's aspirations. By formalising a shared vision, it enabled ASEAN to evolve into a cohesive and resilient regional bloc, paving the way for subsequent initiatives that would define its role in Southeast Asia.

1976: Treaty of Amity and Cooperation

The TAC, signed in 1976 alongside the ASEAN Concord I, was a defining moment in ASEAN's diplomatic journey. It established the core principles guiding ASEAN's interactions within the region and with external partners. Mutual respect for sovereignty and territorial integrity became a hallmark of the Association's diplomacy, ensuring that each member's borders and domestic affairs were respected. This principle was crucial for a region historically marked by external interference and colonial legacies.

The treaty further entrenched the principle of non-interference in member states' internal affairs. ASEAN members committed to refraining from meddling in each other's domestic politics, allowing the organisation to focus on shared interests rather than internal disputes. The TAC also emphasised the importance of peaceful dispute resolution, encouraging dialogue, mediation, and negotiation as the preferred means for handling regional tensions.

What made the TAC particularly significant was its reach beyond ASEAN's borders. Over the years, many external powers, including China, Japan, India, the United States, Russia and the European Union, became signatories to the treaty. As of October 2024, there are 54 signatories to the TAC. This includes both ASEAN member states and various non-ASEAN countries that came to join it over the years. The most recent countries to accede to the treaty are Luxembourg, Panama, Serbia, and Kuwait, who signed the agreement during the ASEAN meetings in 2023 and 2024.

The TAC has expanded beyond its original purpose of fostering peace and cooperation within Southeast Asia to become a global framework for peaceful international relations. It now includes countries from Southeast Asia, East Asia, South Asia, Oceania, Europe, North America, Latin America, and Africa. This global acknowledgement highlights the importance of ASEAN in regional and international diplomacy and affirms its role as a hub for peaceful cooperation in Southeast Asia.

1971: Zone of Peace, Freedom, and Neutrality

The ZOPFAN declaration of 1971 was ASEAN's first significant foray into shaping regional security. At the height of the Cold War, Southeast Asian countries were at risk of being drawn into the superpower rivalries between the United States, the Soviet Union, and China. ZOPFAN was ASEAN's statement to the world: Southeast Asia would remain a neutral zone, free from interference by any external powers.

The declaration called for the region's autonomy and emphasised the importance of peaceful coexistence.

ZOPFAN aimed to establish Southeast Asia as a region where disputes would be managed internally and resolved without outside influence, ensuring that regional security was a shared ASEAN responsibility. While ZOPFAN was largely aspirational, it laid the groundwork for later security initiatives, such as the ASEAN Regional Forum (ARF) and the Southeast Asia Nuclear-Weapon-Free Zone Treaty (SEANFWZ), cementing ASEAN's role in fostering peace and stability.

1995: Southeast Asia Nuclear-Weapon-Free Zone Treaty

Building on ZOPFAN's vision of a neutral and peaceful Southeast Asia, the SEANWFZ Treaty was signed in 1995, formalising ASEAN's commitment to keeping the region free from nuclear weapons. The treaty prohibits the development, acquisition, testing, and use of nuclear weapons in Southeast Asia, marking a significant step toward promoting peace and security in the region. SEANWFZ includes mechanisms for verifying compliance and underscores ASEAN's commitment to the peaceful use of nuclear technology. While challenges remain in getting nuclear-armed states to sign on to the protocol to respect the zone, SEANWFZ stands as a key pillar of ASEAN's dedication to regional security and aligns with global efforts toward disarmament and non-proliferation.

The nuclear powers have yet to sign the SEANWFZ Treaty due to concerns about strategic and operational limitations. Key issues include restrictions on freedom of navigation and overflight for nuclear-armed vessels and aircraft, which could affect their military flexibility. Additionally, nuclear powers are reluctant due to extended deterrence policies, particularly the United States, which relies on nuclear deployments to guarantee the security of allies in the region. Ambiguities regarding the treaty's application to territorial waters and verification mechanisms also pose challenges.

To date, only China has come close to signing the Treaty. In the early 2000s, China indicated a willingness to engage in discussions with ASEAN regarding the treaty and sign protocols that would affirm its commitment to a nuclear-free Southeast Asia. However, concerns over the treaty's interpretation of freedom of navigation and including international waters have kept China from finalising its accession. Other nuclear powers, such as the United States, Russia, and France, have also been engaged in discussions but have not come as close as China to signing.

1997: ASEAN Vision 2020

By 1997, ASEAN had begun looking beyond its immediate challenges and laying a long-term foundation for its future by adopting the ASEAN Vision 2020. This forward-looking document articulated an ambitious goal: to transform Southeast Asia into a cohesive and concerted region that could serve as an effective force for peace, justice, and moderation. The vision called for a stable, prosperous, and highly competitive ASEAN economic region, characterised by the free flow of goods, services, and capital, all underpinned by a shared regional identity.

A cornerstone of the vision was deeper economic integration, which laid the groundwork for developing the ASEAN Economic Community (AEC). By emphasising collaboration in trade, investment, and economic policies, the document positioned ASEAN as a significant player in the global economy. At the same time, it reaffirmed ASEAN's commitment to regional peace and stability, underscoring the importance of non-interference, conflict prevention, and peaceful dispute resolution. Beyond economics and security, ASEAN Vision 2020 envisioned a caring and cohesive community, one that fosters social development, strengthens cultural ties, and enhances the quality of life for its people.

This transformative document was a defining moment in ASEAN's journey, shaping its policies and integration efforts for decades to come. Its principles and aspirations have continued to guide ASEAN's initiatives, including formally establishing the ASEAN Community in 2015, making it a key milestone in the organisation's evolution.

2003: ASEAN Concord II

The ASEAN Concord II, also referred to as the Bali Concord II, was a transformative milestone in ASEAN's history when it was signed in October 2003. This landmark agreement formalised the vision for creating the ASEAN Community, laying the groundwork for deeper integration across its member states. The Concord established three key pillars: the ASEAN Political-Security Community (APSC), the ASEAN Economic Community (AEC), and the ASEAN Socio-Cultural Community (ASCC). These pillars have since become the foundation of ASEAN's community efforts to promote regional peace, prosperity, and cohesion.

The APSC aimed to deepen political and security cooperation, emphasising the importance of conflict prevention and peaceful dispute resolution. It sought to build trust and transparency through the Treaty of Amity and Cooperation (TAC) and promote a rules-based regional order. Initiatives under this pillar included enhancing defence diplomacy and counterterrorism efforts, reflecting the growing need for collective action against transnational challenges, such as the 2001 regional terrorism concerns following the 9/11 attacks.

The AEC, inspired by the European Union's single market model but adapted to ASEAN's unique circumstances, envisioned a highly competitive economic region. Its goals included the free flow of goods, services, investment, and skilled labour, alongside the freer movement of capital. The Concord introduced the idea of ASEAN as a single production base, aiming to attract foreign investment and increase global competitiveness. By 2015, key agreements such as the ASEAN Free Trade Area (AFTA) had contributed significantly to these goals, although challenges in harmonising regulations and addressing disparities among member economies persisted.

The ASCC highlighted the importance of fostering a people-centred and socially responsible ASEAN. This pillar aimed to improve citizens' quality of life by focusing on education, social welfare, environmental sustainability, and cultural preservation. Efforts like the ASEAN Declaration on Environmental Sustainability (2007) and initiatives for disaster response through the ASEAN Agreement on Disaster Management and Emergency Response (AADMER) underscored the region's commitment to addressing shared vulnerabilities.

Together, these pillars signified ASEAN's shift toward a more structured and cohesive organisation, culminating in the formal establishment of the ASEAN Community in 2015. The Bali Concord II was pivotal in redefining ASEAN's role, ensuring it remains central to addressing regional challenges while pursuing global opportunities.

2007: The ASEAN Charter

Adopting the ASEAN Charter in November 2007 marked a transformative moment in ASEAN's history, turning it into a rules-based entity with legal standing and granting it international legal personality. This shift allowed ASEAN to enter into treaties, enforce its decisions, and better manage regional and international relations. The Charter introduced core values such as democracy, human rights, and good governance, underscoring ASEAN's commitment to addressing internal governance challenges.

Crucially, the Charter institutionalised ASEAN's frameworks, establishing clearer decision-making processes and dispute-resolution mechanisms. This paved the way for deeper integration, including the launch of the ASEAN Community in 2015, which was structured around three pillars: APSC, AEC, and ASCC. These pillars collectively aimed to strengthen regional stability, economic integration, and sociocultural ties, solidifying ASEAN's relevance in a globalised world. The Charter provided the legal and institutional foundation for these ambitious community-building efforts by formalising ASEAN's structure.

The Charter strengthened ASEAN's external relations, consolidating its role in platforms like the ASEAN Plus Three (APT), East Asia Summit (EAS), and ASEAN Post-Ministerial Conferences (PMCs) and its participation in global platforms. It enhanced the authority of the Secretary-General and established the Committee of Permanent Representatives (CPRs) to ensure coordination among member states. The Charter maintained ASEAN's core principles of non-interference and sovereignty while still allowing flexible decision-making to preserve regional unity amidst diversity.

Tools such as the ASEAN minus X formula for implementing agreed-upon economic initiatives, the expanded role of the Secretary-General, and formal dispute-resolution processes have allowed ASEAN to progress on key initiatives without compromising its principles. This balance of tradition and innovation has enabled ASEAN to remain unified and resilient in navigating regional and global complexities while advancing its vision for a peaceful, stable, and integrated Southeast Asia.

2011: ASEAN Concord III

The Bali Declaration on ASEAN Community in a Global Community of Nations (Bali Concord III), adopted in November 2011, reaffirmed ASEAN's commitment to peace, security, and sustainable development while strengthening its global engagement. It highlighted ASEAN's adherence to fundamental principles such as sovereignty, territorial integrity, and non-interference and its dedication to addressing transnational challenges like counterterrorism, maritime security, and nuclear disarmament. The declaration also emphasised ASEAN's central role in fostering regional cooperation and enhancing its ability to respond to global issues through a stronger ASEAN Secretariat.

The declaration outlined key priorities across three areas: political-security, economic, and socio-cultural cooperation. Politically, ASEAN aimed to promote peace, settle disputes peacefully, and combat transnational crimes. Economically, it sought to enhance trade, ensure financial stability, and promote inclusive and sustainable growth. Socio-culturally, the focus was on disaster management, climate change adaptation, and improving access to healthcare, education, and fair working conditions. These efforts aligned with global frameworks like the Millennium Development Goals and aimed to position ASEAN as a proactive partner in addressing global challenges.

ASEAN leaders were committed to raising the region's global profile and strengthening its voice in international forums such as the United Nations. They pledged to enhance cooperation on global issues and adapt to changing global dynamics.

Indonesia's role in ASEAN

Indonesia's importance in ASEAN is deeply rooted in its role as a founding member and its consistent and balanced leadership in shaping the organisation's policies and direction. As Southeast Asia's largest country in terms of population, economy, and geography, Indonesia has served as the de facto leader, ensuring ASEAN remains a platform for dialogue, cooperation, and regional stability. From its active role in shaping the Bangkok Declaration, which established ASEAN, to its leadership in crafting subsequent frameworks such as the Treaty of Amity and Cooperation (TAC), Indonesia has been a steadfast proponent of peaceful conflict resolution, sovereignty, and regional unity. These principles have become the foundation of ASEAN's diplomatic and political ethos.

Indonesia has consistently acted as ASEAN's consensus-builder, navigating diverse member-state interests while promoting regional integration. For example, during the Cambodian conflict in the 1980s, Indonesia played a critical role in facilitating negotiations and hosting peace talks that eventually led to Cambodia's integration into ASEAN. Similarly, Indonesia's leadership during the 2003 ASEAN Summit in Bali resulted in the adoption of Bali Concord II, which laid the groundwork for the ASEAN Community, emphasising integration across political-security, economic, and socio-cultural pillars. This initiative highlighted Indonesia's vision for a united ASEAN capable of addressing regional challenges effectively.

Indonesia has championed the development of the ASEAN Political Security Community (APSC) and played an influential role in the creation of the ASEAN Economic Community (AEC), reinforcing ASEAN's position as a competitive and integrated economic bloc. Its push for inclusivity in these frameworks ensures that all member states benefit from economic integration regardless of their development level. Furthermore, Indonesia's proactive stance on global issues, evident in Bali Concord III (2011), underscores its vision of ASEAN as a globally influential entity. By emphasising the need for ASEAN to play a constructive role in addressing transnational challenges like climate change, terrorism, and nuclear disarmament, Indonesia has solidified its position as a collaborative leader that drives ASEAN's strategic relevance both regionally and globally.

In short, ASEAN's evolution through its core documents showcases an organisation adept at balancing its founding principles with the demands of an ever-changing geopolitical landscape. From the Bangkok

Declaration to the ASEAN Charter, each legal and strategic framework has been crucial in cementing ASEAN's commitment to regional peace, stability, and economic growth. As ASEAN tackles 21st-century challenges, its foundational principles—respect for sovereignty, non-interference, and regional cooperation—will continue to guide its efforts to remain a resilient, dynamic, and influential force in regional affairs. By balancing flexibility and adherence to its core values, ASEAN is well-positioned to address emerging challenges and opportunities in an increasingly complex world.

> *"ASEAN's core documents, from the Bangkok Declaration to the ASEAN Charter, provide the legal and institutional framework that has enabled ASEAN to evolve from a loosely formed association of countries into a fully-fledged regional organisation. These documents are the backbone of ASEAN's collective vision for peace, security, and economic cooperation."*
>
> **Pushpanathan Sundram, Author**

Chapter 3

The ASEAN Charter – Formalising Regional Unity

"The ASEAN Charter will serve the organisation well in three interrelated ways, such as formally according to ASEAN legal personality, establishing greater institutional accountability and compliance system, and reinforcing the perception of ASEAN as a serious regional player in the future of the Asia Pacific region."

ASEAN Secretary-General Ong Keng Yong at the signing of the ASEAN Charter, 13th ASEAN Summit, Singapore, November 20, 2007

For more than four decades, ASEAN's strength lay in its informality—an organisation driven by dialogue, consensus, and a shared sense of regional identity. This approach allowed ASEAN to grow flexibly, adapting to challenges and raising cooperation. But as the organisation matured, so did the complexity of its ambitions. The expansion of ASEAN's scope, the need for deeper economic integration, and the growing demands for regional influence made it clear that an informal structure could only take it so far. The organisation needed something more: a framework that could consolidate and empower it, so the idea of a formal charter began to take form.

In November 2007, this vision became a reality with the adoption of the ASEAN Charter. This transformative document turned ASEAN from a loosely knit diplomatic forum into a rules-based, legally binding regional grouping. This chapter will take you through the journey to the Charter, break down its key provisions, and study its impact on ASEAN's emerging role in regional and global governance. It will also show how the Charter contributed to creating a more people-oriented ASEAN, bringing citizens and civil society closer to the core of ASEAN's mission.

Road to the ASEAN Charter

By the late 1990s and early 2000s, it was becoming increasingly evident that ASEAN needed a more robust legal foundation. The traditional approach of informal diplomacy, consensus-building, and non-interference had helped ASEAN circumnavigate tricky waters, but as the organisation began to pursue more ambitious projects, like the AEC, it became clear that these informal structures had limitations. Leaders and policymakers alike recognised that deeper integration and a larger international footprint would require stronger institutional mechanisms.

In 1997, the adoption of ASEAN Vision 2020 marked a turning point, laying out a strategic path for a more integrated and dynamic ASEAN. This long-term vision called for greater political and economic cooperation, a shared regional identity, and a role for ASEAN on the international stage. However, to bring this vision to life, ASEAN needed more than just ideals; it required a solid legal and institutional foundation.

That push came with the ASEAN Concord II in 2003. This document paved the way for the three pillars of the ASEAN Community, underscoring the need for a comprehensive legal and institutional framework. By 2005, momentum was building rapidly for a formal charter, and the member states formed a High-Level Task Force to draft the ASEAN Charter, following recommendations from the ASEAN Charter Eminent Persons Group. This task force, composed of representatives from all ten ASEAN countries, had one mission: to create a document that would not only formalise ASEAN's legal status but also give the organisation the institutional mechanisms it needed to thrive as an effective regional Association.

Attending some of the ASEAN eminent persons group and the high-level task force discussions on the ASEAN Charter, I witnessed firsthand the balancing act between upholding the organisation's foundational principles and addressing the political realities member states face. The high-level task force acknowledged the need to embed democratic values and human rights into the Charter while retaining ASEAN's traditional emphasis on non-interference and respect for sovereignty. This highlighted how important it was to position ASEAN as a relevant player on the international stage without compromising its core tenets.

During these sessions of the eminent persons group and the high-level task force, it became apparent that each member played a pivotal role in shaping the Charter. With their extensive experience and high standing in their respective countries, the eminent persons pushed for a progressive vision for ASEAN, advocating for a structured legal framework to empower the organisation. Meanwhile, the high-level task force worked diligently to ensure that these recommendations aligned with ASEAN's existing principles and framework, facilitating a smooth integration of new ideas.

This dynamic exchange reflected a significant evolution in ASEAN's approach, marking a crucial transition towards a more robust governance structure. It was a complex but essential process to enhance ASEAN's engagement with the international community and lay the groundwork for a more cohesive and caring ASEAN. This journey was not just about drafting a document. It was about envisioning the future of ASEAN and fostering a sense of ownership among member states in an intergovernmental setting.

ASEAN Charter key provisions

The Charter was officially signed on November 20, 2007, during the 13th ASEAN Summit in Singapore, and it came into effect on December 15, 2008. This historic move marked a new chapter for ASEAN, transforming it into a rules-based organisation with clear legal standing. The Charter codified ASEAN's core principles, created new institutions, and provided dispute resolution, decision-making, and enforcement mechanisms. One of the Charter's most significant achievements was granting ASEAN a legal personality, effectively empowering it to enter into international agreements, negotiate treaties, and engage with external partners as an entity. This legal status enhanced ASEAN's diplomatic credibility, allowing it to play a more active role in international forums alongside major powers like the United States, China, Japan, and the European Union.

The Charter established several institutional mechanisms to enhance governance and decision-making processes within ASEAN. The ASEAN Summit was formalised as the organisation's highest policy-making and decision-making body, with leaders of member states meeting at least twice a year to set strategic directions and tackle regional issues. To ensure the decisions of the Summit were implemented effectively, the Charter created the ASEAN Coordinating Council (ACC), composed primarily of foreign ministers, to oversee the work across the organisation's three pillars. The Charter established three community councils corresponding to the ASEAN Community's pillars: APSC, AEC, and ASCC. A Committee of Permanent Representatives (CPRs) was also created primarily to oversee and ensure the implementation of decisions made by ASEAN Leaders, coordinating cross-community pillar issues, enhancing external relations and providing guidance and support to the ASEAN Secretariat's functions.

The Charter enhanced the administrative role of the ASEAN Secretariat to support the effective functioning of new and existing ASEAN mechanisms by facilitating communication between member states and monitoring the implementation of agreements and initiatives. The Charter formalised the position of the ASEAN Secretary-General at the ministerial rank, appointed by the ASEAN Summit for a fixed five-year term to serve as the Chief Administrative Officer overseeing ASEAN's operations. The Secretary-General is supported by four Deputy Secretaries-General (DSGs) at the Deputy Minister rank, each responsible for key areas: political security, economic, socio-cultural, and community and corporate affairs.

Significantly, the Charter introduced new commitments to human rights, democracy, and good governance, which was previously considered too sensitive for ASEAN's non-interference approach. The establishment of the ASEAN Intergovernmental Commission on Human Rights (AICHR) marked a milestone, making it the first time human rights were institutionalised within the ASEAN framework. While

AICHR's role is primarily advisory, its creation signalled ASEAN's recognition of human rights as an important aspect of its broader mission. The Charter formalised mechanisms for peaceful dispute resolution. While ASEAN traditionally relied on dialogue and diplomacy, the Charter introduced clearer mediation, conciliation, and arbitration processes. This legal framework ensured that member-state disputes could be addressed constructively, maintaining regional stability and trust.

Principles, norms, and values of ASEAN: A clearer perspective

In discussions about ASEAN, the terms principles, norms, and values are often used interchangeably, leading to confusion even among scholars and policymakers. What do these terms truly mean in the ASEAN context? How are they distinct, and why do they matter? I attempt to provide clarity, cutting through decades of ambiguity surrounding these concepts.

ASEAN's principles are formal, legally binding commitments. These rules are codified in foundational documents like the Treaty of Amity and Cooperation (TAC) and the ASEAN Charter. Principles serve as the legal framework that governs how ASEAN member states engage with one another. For example, the TAC introduced key principles like non-interference in domestic affairs, the peaceful settlement of disputes, and the renunciation of force, which were crucial for ensuring stability in a region emerging from colonialism and Cold

War rivalries. These principles were later expanded and codified in the ASEAN Charter, creating a more structured and predictable basis for ASEAN's governance.

In contrast, norms are informal practices that have evolved organically from Southeast Asia's political and cultural realities. They are unwritten but deeply ingrained in ASEAN's operational style, such as consensus decision-making and non-confrontation. These norms were moulded by a shared preference for dialogue, gradual progress, and harmony rather than rigid enforcement or confrontational politics. Over time, some norms have been institutionalised in the Charter as a principle, demonstrating how ASEAN balances informality with legal structure.

Values, on the other hand, reflect the shared beliefs and ideals that underpin ASEAN's principles and norms. These include respect for sovereignty, regional stability, and unity in diversity. Values provide the moral compass that guides ASEAN's actions, ensuring that its decisions align with the collective aspirations of its member states.

The adoption of the ASEAN Charter in 2007 was a turning point, as it formalised and expanded ASEAN's principles into a legally binding framework. This codification brought much-needed clarity to ASEAN's foundational rules, reducing ambiguity and reinforcing the organisation's legitimacy. The Charter lists the following principles in Article 2(2), which reflect ASEAN's commitments to peace, stability, and cooperation:

1. **Respect for Sovereignty and Identity:** Independence, sovereignty, equality, territorial integrity, and national identity of all Member States.
2. **Regional Peace and Responsibility:** Shared commitment and collective responsibility for regional peace, security, and prosperity.
3. **Non-Aggression:** Renunciation of aggression and actions inconsistent with international law.
4. **Peaceful Dispute Resolution:** Settling disputes through peaceful means.
5. **Non-Interference:** Commitment to non-interference in the internal affairs of Member States.
6. **Freedom from External Influence:** Respect for each Member State's right to exist without external interference or coercion.
7. **Enhanced Consultation:** Dialogue and consultations on matters of common interest.
8. **Rule of Law and Governance:** Adherence to the rule of law, democracy, good governance, and constitutional government.
9. **Human Rights and Social Justice:** Promotion and protection of fundamental freedoms, human rights, and social justice.
10. **Adherence to International Norms:** Commitment to the UN Charter, international law, and humanitarian principles.
11. **Sovereignty and Stability:** Avoidance of policies or activities that threaten the sovereignty or stability of Member States.
12. **Unity in Diversity:** Respect for the region's diverse cultures, languages, and religions, emphasising common values and unity.

13. **ASEAN Centrality:** Maintaining ASEAN's central role in external relations while being outward-looking, inclusive, and non-discriminatory.
14. **Multilateral Trade Rules:** Adherence to multilateral trade rules and progressive elimination of barriers to regional integration.
15. **Rules-Based Implementation:** Commitment to ASEAN's rules-based regimes to effectively implement economic and other commitments.

The codification of these principles has been instrumental in providing ASEAN with a unified legal framework. It clarified the obligations of member states and ensured that ASEAN's actions were consistent with its foundational commitments. Importantly, it has strengthened ASEAN's identity as a rules-based organisation, elevating its standing in global diplomacy.

The codification of principles in the Charter has helped bridge the gap between ASEAN's legal commitments and operational practices. While principles provide the structure and predictability needed for cooperation, norms allow flexibility and adaptability in navigating ASEAN's diversity. For instance, consensus decision-making, a norm rooted in cultural tradition, was formally institutionalised in the Charter (Article 20), ensuring that member states continue to feel included in decision-making.

At the same time, ASEAN's values—its commitment to sovereignty, stability, and cooperation—remain the moral foundation of its actions. These values reinforce the trust and unity that underpin ASEAN's principles and norms, making the organisation more resilient in addressing both internal and external challenges.

By formalising its principles in the Charter and balancing them with informal norms and shared values, ASEAN has created a distinctive framework for regional cooperation. This framework is not only functional but reflective of the region's evolving political, cultural, and historical realities. The "ASEAN Way"—a careful balance of legal obligations, informal practices, and shared ideals—continues to be a model of how regional organisations can adapt to diversity while maintaining cohesion.

ASEAN minus X formula

The ASEAN minus X implementation formula emerged as a strategic response to the diverse economic landscapes and varying readiness levels among ASEAN member states. This approach permits a subset of countries to advance with specific economic initiatives, allowing others to join when ready. The formula was formalised in the ASEAN Charter under Article 21(2), which states: "In the implementation of economic commitments, a formula for flexible participation, including the ASEAN Minus X formula, may be applied where there is a consensus to do so."

The formula has been instrumental in facilitating economic integration within the ASEAN Economic Community (AEC) framework. It enables member states that are prepared for deeper economic cooperation to proceed without being hindered by those less prepared. This flexibility has been particularly beneficial in areas such as trade liberalisation and services integration. For example, the formula has been applied in implementing the ASEAN Single Aviation Market (ASAM), allowing participating countries to advance in liberalising air services while others prepare to join later.

The formula accommodates the varying capacities of its members, ensuring that the region's economic integration progresses. This approach maintains ASEAN's unity and inclusivity, allowing for collective progress while respecting individual member states' readiness and capabilities.

The ASEAN minus X formula can offer a flexible and pragmatic approach that can be extended to other ASEAN communities for less sensitive issues. For instance, in the ASEAN Political Security Community (APSC), this formula could be applied to accelerate cooperation on counter-terrorism, cybersecurity, or disaster management, allowing willing states to lead while others build capacity. Similarly, in the ASEAN Socio-Cultural Community (ASCC), member states prepared to implement regional policies on climate change adaptation or public health initiatives could move forward, setting benchmarks for others to follow. Using this formula across ASEAN's pillars, the organisation can ensure progress in addressing urgent regional challenges while maintaining inclusivity and unity, fostering a balance between ambition and readiness.

Towards a people-oriented ASEAN

The ASEAN Charter underscored the organisation's commitment to becoming more people-oriented and people-centred. It laid the groundwork for greater engagement with various affiliated entities, from youth and civil society groups to the private sector and professional associations. These entities, including the ASEAN Foundation, the ASEAN Youth Organisation, and the ASEAN Inter-Parliamentary Assembly (AIPA), play a critical role in realising ASEAN's vision of inclusive, participatory governance.

The ASEAN Foundation, for instance, focuses on building ASEAN awareness and collaboration among the region's citizens. It promotes education, culture, and social development initiatives and supports efforts to reduce poverty and build human resources. The ASEAN Youth Organisation engages the region's young population, recognising that the future of ASEAN lies in its youth. The organisation fosters a sense of regional identity and active youth participation by organising educational programs, leadership workshops, and exchanges.

The AIPA, an affiliated entity under the Charter, serves as a platform for legislators from ASEAN member states to engage in dialogue and share best practices on governance, laws, and regional issues. This assembly supports bridging ASEAN's intergovernmental processes with national legislatures, making the organisation more inclusive and representative of its people.

The ASEAN Business Advisory Council (ABAC) and business councils formed with dialogue partners like the United States, European Union, Japan, and India created a bridge between ASEAN's economic policies and private sector interests. These councils allow for business input on economic integration and policy matters. Civil society groups also have a voice through platforms like the ASEAN Civil Society Conference (ACSC) and the ASEAN People's Forum (APF), which engage with leaders on issues ranging from labour rights to environmental protection.

ASEAN Charter and ASEAN Community

The adoption of the ASEAN Charter marked a key milestone in shaping the ASEAN Community, which officially came into existence in 2015. The Charter's legal framework is the foundation for the Community's three main pillars: political-security collaboration, economic integration, and social advancement. These are embodied by the ASEAN Political-Security Community (APSC), the ASEAN Economic Community (AEC), and the ASEAN Socio-Cultural Community (ASCC).

The APSC centres on promoting peace, safeguarding regional security, and averting conflicts. The Charter's focus on dialogue and systems for resolving disputes has been crucial in meeting these aims, providing ASEAN with the means to address regional tensions more effectively.

The AEC works towards building a single market and production base by encouraging the unrestricted movement of goods, services, capital, and skilled labour. The governance framework established by the Charter has supported ASEAN in implementing significant measures in trade and investment, driving economic development and enhancing regional links.

At the same time, the ASCC focuses on advancing social welfare, safeguarding human rights, supporting environmental sustainability, and fostering a collective cultural identity. The Charter's dedication to democracy, human rights, and sound governance aligns with the ASCC's goals, encouraging a more inclusive and united ASEAN community.

ASEAN secretariat: sovereignty or coordination and execution

The Charter recognised the Secretariat as the primary entity to support ASEAN's growing regional agenda, emphasising its importance in facilitating the integration process. As the focal point for ASEAN's activities, the Secretariat is responsible for providing administrative support, coordinating various programs, and assisting in implementing policies and initiatives agreed upon by member states. The Secretary-General of ASEAN, appointed for a fixed term, is identified as the Chief

Administrative Officer of the Secretariat, reflecting the body's primary function as an administrative entity.

Despite its increased responsibilities, the Charter clarified that the Secretariat was designed to operate as an administrative secretariat without decision-making powers or independent authority over policy. This decision was driven by ASEAN's key principles of sovereignty, non-interference, and consensus-based decision-making. As an intergovernmental organisation, ASEAN emphasised that member states retain control over policy and decision-making, and the Secretariat's role was to support and facilitate, not lead or drive policy direction. Therefore, it was clear that an independent Secretariat could pose conflicts in decision-making.

In order to avoid such issues, the Charter drafters explored the possibility of different secretariat models, assessing how the Secretariat could best serve ASEAN's needs. However, member states were clear in choosing an administrative model prioritising support over coordination or execution. The coordinating secretariat model, which would allow a more active role in aligning policies and promoting regional programs, was seen as too intrusive. Similarly, the executive secretariat model, like that of the European Commission, which would give the Secretariat significant autonomy and policy enforcement powers, was dismissed as incompatible with ASEAN's principles.

As the Deputy Secretary-General of ASEAN from 2009 to 2011, I experienced firsthand the constant challenge of managing the Secretariat's expanding roles with its limited resources. During my tenure, we worked closely with the CPRs of ASEAN, who represented the interests of the respective ASEAN countries, to address the Secretariat's capacity constraints while delivering on the growing responsibilities and expectations placed on ASEAN. The Secretariat faced significant hurdles in meeting the increasing demand for policy support, coordination, and implementation while operating with limited financial and human resources.

One key challenge was ensuring that the Secretariat had the human resource capacity to support ASEAN's ambitious initiatives, especially with the advent of the ASEAN Charter and the ASEAN community blueprints, which formalised and expanded the Secretariat's responsibilities. Despite these new roles, the Secretariat's status as an administrative body limited its ability to influence policies proactively. Consequently, we were often stretched thin, tasked with facilitating numerous meetings, managing regional programs, and supporting coordination across sectors.

The CPRs played a critical role during this time, serving as a bridge between the Secretariat and national governments, advocating for better support and resources. However, it was always a delicate balance. Member states were wary of granting too much autonomy or an executive role that might infringe on their sovereignty. One discussion with the CPRs stands out in my memory, during which the idea of evolving towards a coordinating secretariat was raised. It was quickly met with firm resistance. One member articulated the sentiment clearly: "We are not the European Union, and we're not going to be." The remark highlighted the shared stance of the member states; they were committed to keeping ASEAN an intergovernmental organisation, and any step toward granting the Secretariat greater power was seen as compromising their sovereignty.

The ASEAN Secretaries General did their part in seeking innovative solutions to the budget crunch. This included practical ideas like a token charge for each traveller passing through ASEAN airports or issuing an ASEAN postage stamp to raise funds. They had to confront the reality of an ever-expanding ASEAN agenda that outpaced the Secretariat's limited resources, striving to ensure that despite these constraints, the Secretariat could effectively support ASEAN's growing ambitions. These attempts were often met with caution by member states who valued the Secretariat's administrative role and were reluctant to see its power and budget significantly expanded, maintaining the focus on intergovernmental cooperation and consensus-building.

Throughout this period, we worked tirelessly to enhance the Secretariat's efficiency. With the CPRs' support, we sought incremental budget increases, optimised the use of resources, and streamlined operations. A crucial part was capacity building—ensuring the Secretariat's staff had the necessary skills, expertise and international exposure to manage ASEAN's growing workload and complexity. Despite structural limitations, these efforts allowed the Secretariat to effectively support the region's integration agenda and ASEAN to achieve its goals across economic, political, and socio-cultural cooperation. Thus, the Secretariat was to support ASEAN's growing agenda by facilitating dialogue and coordination, but without holding any independent power to ensure compliance and enforce policies, thereby upholding the values of sovereignty, consensus, and mutual respect among its members.

ASEAN Charter in practice

While the ASEAN Charter has been a robust framework, its principles have faced real-world tests. The South China Sea dispute, the Rohingya crisis in Myanmar, and the Thailand-Cambodia Border Conflict are three prominent examples.

The ongoing South China Sea dispute has tested the Charter's commitment to peaceful dispute resolution and regional cooperation. With overlapping territorial claims among ASEAN member states and China's expansive Nine-Dash Line, the situation is fraught with geopolitical tensions. The Charter's principles of dialogue and consensus-building have guided ASEAN's approach, leading to agreements like the Declaration on the Conduct of Parties in the South China Sea (DOC). However, the DOC's non-binding nature has limited its effectiveness, and efforts to develop a legally binding Code of Conduct in the South China Sea (COC) have faced obstacles.

Key challenges to the COC include China's insistence on provisions limiting military exercises with external powers unless Beijing is notified and agrees. ASEAN claimant countries have opposed these provisions, which they see as limiting their sovereign rights. Furthermore, China has also proposed that oil and gas exploration in disputed areas be conducted only through cooperation among the littoral states, excluding foreign companies. This has also faced resistance from ASEAN claimant countries, which argue for the right to collaborate with foreign partners under international law.

Despite these differences, ASEAN leaders have called for the early conclusion of the COC, emphasising its importance for regional stability. However, the deep divisions among ASEAN members and China's reluctance to compromise have made it challenging to achieve substantive progress, thereby impacting the Charter's aim of promoting peace and cooperation due to geopolitical realities.

The ASEAN Charter's principles on peaceful dispute resolution were again tested during the Thailand-Cambodia border conflict over the Preah Vihear Temple from 2008 to 2011. The dispute centred around the land surrounding the temple, with tensions escalating in 2008 after UNESCO listed the temple as a World Heritage Site under Cambodia, sparking armed clashes.

The dispute between Thailand and Cambodia exemplified ASEAN's delicate balancing act in mediating regional conflicts. Rooted in ambiguous territorial claims stemming from a 1962 ICJ ruling, tensions escalated into violent clashes from 2008 to 2011. ASEAN, led by Indonesia as Chair, employed its hallmark "ASEAN Way" diplomacy, which emphasises consensus, non-interference, and peaceful resolution of disputes. Indonesian Foreign Minister Marty Natalegawa spearheaded shuttle diplomacy, facilitating dialogues between the two nations, while ASEAN deployed neutral observers to stabilise the border.

These efforts, complemented by the ICJ's clarification in 2013, established a demilitarised zone, defused tensions, and paved the way for military withdrawals and peaceful negotiations. While ASEAN's informal approach revealed its structural limitations in enforcing resolutions, its role in fostering dialogue and leveraging international mechanisms underscored its importance as a stabilising force in Southeast Asia.

The recent Rohingya crisis in Myanmar is another case where the Charter's principles have faced scrutiny. The mass displacement of Rohingya Muslims and human rights violations have raised questions about ASEAN's commitment to human rights and its principle of non-interference. While ASEAN has provided humanitarian assistance, advocated for safe refugee return, and appointed special envoys, criticism has followed regarding the limited influence and perceived lack of action on Myanmar's internal issues.

The ASEAN Five-Point Consensus, adopted in April 2021 in response to the military coup in Myanmar, remains the main framework for ASEAN's efforts to resolve the political crisis and the Rohingya situation, even though the Consensus is not directly related to the latter issue. The consensus outlines the cessation of violence, constructive dialogue among all parties, the appointment of a Special Envoy to mediate discussions, humanitarian assistance, and a visit by the Special Envoy to Myanmar to meet all stakeholders. However, the implementation has faced significant challenges. Despite ASEAN's repeated calls, violence continues in Myanmar, and the military junta has been resistant to fully implementing the consensus. ASEAN leaders have expressed concern about the lack of progress and have urged more concrete action from all parties involved.

So far, three Special Envoys have been appointed based on the rotation of ASEAN chairmanship. They are Brunei's Foreign Minister, Erywan Yusof, in 2021, Cambodian Foreign Minister Prakash Sokhonn, in 2022 and former Minister in the Lao Prime Minister's Office, Alounkeo Kittikhoun, in 2024. The first envoy initiated a dialogue between Myanmar's military and opposition forces. However, his efforts faced resistance from the junta. The second envoy continued the efforts, but the junta's lack of cooperation has limited his progress. Similarly, the third envoy faced obstacles in gaining cooperation from the junta.

The ongoing challenges in Myanmar have highlighted the limitations of ASEAN's rotating special envoy system, which has struggled to achieve meaningful progress due to inconsistent engagement and varying diplomatic approaches. Perhaps appointing a full-time, permanent Special Envoy for Myanmar to address this could ensure sustained and cohesive efforts, allowing for continuous dialogue with all stakeholders and a more consistent application of ASEAN's Five-Point Consensus. This approach could enhance ASEAN's credibility and effectiveness in facilitating a peaceful resolution to the crisis.

In essence, the ASEAN Charter has been a transformative milestone, equipping the organisation with the legal and institutional tools to pursue deeper integration and a more active regional role. Its principles of consensus, respect for sovereignty, and commitment to human rights have laid a foundation for ASEAN's continued growth and relevance. Yet, the Charter's challenges, particularly in human rights and dispute resolution, reveal areas where ASEAN must evolve.

As ASEAN nears the conclusion of its 2025 Blueprints, the organisation has embarked on a comprehensive review of the ASEAN Charter in the context of preparing for its Post-2025 Vision. This process is being spearheaded by the High-Level Task Force on ASEAN Community Vision Post-2025 (HLTF-ACV), which has been tasked with ensuring ASEAN's institutional framework remains robust and adaptable to emerging challenges. The review aligns closely with the broader ASEAN Community Vision 2025, aiming to address gaps in implementation and identify reforms that will enhance ASEAN's effectiveness and relevance in an evolving regional and global environment.

The HLTF-ACV has been working alongside the Eminent Persons Group (EPG) to assess the Charter comprehensively. While the EPG provides strategic, high-level recommendations for improving ASEAN's legal and institutional frameworks, the HLTF-ACV translates these into actionable proposals and amendments. This review takes place in the context of regional challenges such as climate change, digital transformation, and geopolitical tensions, focusing on strengthening ASEAN centrality, decision-making processes, and inclusivity. The HLTF-ACV's work will directly influence ASEAN's roadmap for the Post-2025 Vision, ensuring that the organisation remains an effective driver of peace, stability, and prosperity in the coming decades.

As ASEAN concludes its review of the Charter, building a framework that ensures the organisation remains agile, inclusive, and future-ready is imperative. This involves enhancing decision-making processes by introducing mechanisms for faster resolutions of non-sensitive issues while retaining consensus for critical matters. The ASEAN Secretariat should be empowered with greater resources and authority to coordinate, monitor, and enforce regional commitments effectively.

Provisions addressing emerging challenges, such as climate change, cybersecurity, and public health, must be integrated into the Charter to reflect contemporary priorities. Greater inclusivity is important, with structured engagement of civil society, industry, think tanks, and youth organisations to ensure diverse voices inform ASEAN's policies. Reinforcing ASEAN's centrality in regional and global affairs, coupled with clear accountability mechanisms to track and report on progress, will strengthen the organisation's credibility. ASEAN can promote peace and cooperation by fostering flexibility in integration while prioritising a people-centred approach, ensuring its continued regional relevance and effectiveness in the post-2025 era.

> *"The ASEAN Charter marked a defining moment in the institutionalisation of ASEAN. It formalised the principles, norms, and rules that had long guided the organisation, transforming ASEAN into a rules-based entity with a legal personality. The Charter is the cornerstone of ASEAN's future, anchoring its commitment to deeper integration and cooperation."*
>
> **Pushpanathan Sundram, Author**

Chapter 4

The ASEAN Economic Community & Regional Economic Integration

"At the 2002 ASEAN Summit in Phnom Penh, Cambodia, and against the advice that the idea would not fly, I floated the vision of an ASEAN Economic Community (AEC) for study by ministers and officials ... The AEC was an attempt to change the tenor of conversation on economic issues in ASEAN and put it on a more positive footing. My hope was that the ASEAN Member States would coalesce around this concept and recognise the opportunities presented by a shared community."

Singapore's Prime Minister Goh Chok Tong, in his essay in ASEAN@50, Volume 1, The ASEAN Journey: Reflection of ASEAN Leaders and Officials, Economic Research Institute of ASEAN and East Asia, October 2017

ASEAN's economic integration journey has been nothing short of revolutionary, with the region becoming globally competitive. The AEC, established in 2015, is a significant step forward in Southeast Asia's commitment to greater economic cooperation. This effort seeks to facilitate the free flow of commodities, services, investment, capital, and skilled labour among its member countries, significantly changing the region's economy. ASEAN imagined a thriving network where firms can trade easily across borders, investments flow freely, and qualified professionals may relocate to where their skills are most required. This chapter will examine the AEC's accomplishments, problems, and ambitious future plans. We will discuss crucial topics such as intra-ASEAN trade, the ASEAN Single Window (ASW), free trade agreements (FTAs), and financial cooperation.

As we progress through the AEC's dynamic workings, you will discover that it serves as a framework for economic integration and a catalyst for growth and innovation, driving Southeast Asia to the world arena. The AEC symbolises its member nations' combined vision of cooperation, increasing competitiveness, and constructing a more prosperous region for all residents.

First AEC Blueprint: laying the groundwork

The AEC Blueprint 2009-2015 served as ASEAN's first comprehensive roadmap, guiding its efforts towards economic integration and aiming to transform the region into a single market and production base. This Blueprint was built around four key pillars that played a crucial role in shaping Southeast Asia's economic landscape.

The first pillar, the Single Market and Production Base, was particularly ambitious. It focused on facilitating the free flow of goods, services, investment, capital, and skilled labour within the region. A notable achievement under this pillar was the elimination of tariffs on 99% of goods traded within ASEAN through the AFTA established in 1992. This liberalisation effectively created a more integrated market by significantly reducing trade barriers and fostering economic exchanges among member states. Moreover, the Blueprint enabled the movement of skilled labour by introducing Mutual Recognition Arrangements (MRAs) for professional sectors such as engineering, architecture, and nursing. These agreements allowed professionals from one ASEAN country to work in others, creating additional economic opportunities and cultivating a skilled labour market across the region.

The second pillar, Competitive Economic Region, concentrated on boosting the region's economic competitiveness through various strategic improvements. ASEAN initiated measures to strengthen intellectual property rights (IPRs), which provided better protection for innovations and encouraged investment in research and development. There was also a concerted emphasis on enhancing competition policies across member states, ensuring markets remained open and fair while discouraging monopolistic practices. To support the seamless movement of goods, services, investment and capital, ASEAN prioritised infrastructure development through the Master Plan on ASEAN Connectivity (MPAC) 2009-2015. This comprehensive initiative aimed to build efficient transportation, energy, and digital infrastructure networks, significantly improving regional trade and investment efficiency.

The third pillar, Equitable Economic Development, was centred on the commitment to ensure that all member countries could benefit from economic integration. Acknowledging the disparities among its members, the Initiative for ASEAN Integration (IAI) adopted in 2000 played a pivotal role in assisting less-developed countries like Cambodia, Laos, Myanmar, and Vietnam (the CLMV countries) in catching up with the more developed economies in the region. This initiative aimed at narrowing the development gap in the region supports capacity-building efforts, infrastructure development, and trade facilitation to enhance the competitiveness of these nations. Small and medium enterprises (SMEs), vital to ASEAN's economic framework, received significant support to promote inclusive growth and provide widespread economic opportunities across all member states.

The fourth pillar, Integration into the Global Economy, aimed to position ASEAN as a major player on the global stage. The region actively pursued FTAs with key external partners, including China, Japan, South Korea, India, Australia, and New Zealand. These FTAs greatly enhanced ASEAN's ability to attract foreign investment, improve market access for its exports, and strengthen the region's global competitiveness. By cultivating robust economic ties with major global economies, ASEAN was able to integrate more deeply into the world economy and enrich its trade and investment landscape.

Importance of open regionalism

Reflecting on my own involvement as the Principal Director of the Bureau of Economic Integration and Finance of the ASEAN Secretariat in drafting the AEC, I vividly recall the initial focus on the first three pillars. As discussions unfolded among our dedicated committee of leading academics and ASEAN experts tasked with assisting the ASEAN Secretariat with the first draft of the AEC Blueprint, it became clear that while these pillars were critical for regional integration, something vital was missing—the need for a fourth pillar that embraced integration into the international economy.

During one of our brainstorming sessions, we had a light bulb moment. We realised that ASEAN should not just be a fortress of member states. Instead, we needed to adopt the philosophy of open regionalism. This approach emphasised engaging with external partners while simultaneously strengthening our internal frameworks. It was about embracing multilateralism, fostering robust economic ties with key global players, enhancing our competitiveness, attracting foreign investment, and driving sustainable growth.

The concept of open regionalism quickly became one of ASEAN's guiding principles, along with the AEC blueprint. We recognised that by working collaboratively with the global community, ASEAN has and could reinforce its position as a vital player in the international marketplace. I can still picture the enthusiasm in the room as we discussed how this philosophy would support ASEAN's industrialisation and economic growth and contribute to peace and stability in the region. This was not just about drafting a document; it was about envisioning a future where ASEAN's success was intertwined with the success of its partners, creating a resilient and thriving Southeast Asia together.

Through these four pillars, the AEC Blueprint 2009-2015 laid a solid foundation for ASEAN's economic integration. It enhanced intra-regional cooperation and global economic participation while promoting equitable growth and regional competitiveness. By the end of 2015, ASEAN had made remarkable progress, with foreign direct investment (FDI) into the region surpassing $120.8 billion and intra-ASEAN trade steadily growing, further amplifying the region's position as a key player in global trade networks.

AEC Blueprint 2025: moving forward

The AEC Blueprint 2025 builds on the achievements of its predecessor, aiming to deepen economic integration, enhance competitiveness, and bolster resilience across ASEAN. This new framework is structured around five key characteristics, reflecting ASEAN's evolving approach to creating a cohesive economic region that is competitive and adaptable to global economic trends.

The first characteristic, a highly integrated and cohesive economy, emphasises improving trade in goods, services, and investments among ASEAN member states. By reducing non-tariff barriers (NTBs) and enhancing regulatory coherence, ASEAN has made strides in fostering seamless intra-regional trade, leading to greater economic integration. By 2022, intra-ASEAN trade accounted for approximately 22% of the region's total trade, valued at over $830.4 billion.

Critical agreements such as the ASEAN Trade in Services Agreement (ATISA) and the ASEAN Agreement on Electronic Commerce have played essential roles in liberalising the services sector and integrating digital trade. ATISA has created a more open and predictable regime for services, while the E-commerce agreement fosters an enabling environment for electronic trade. Together, these initiatives reflect ASEAN's commitment to advancing traditional and digital trade, setting the stage for a more efficient and inclusive economic landscape.

The second characteristic, a competitive, innovative, and dynamic ASEAN, aims to foster an environment conducive to entrepreneurship, innovation, and adopting new technologies. Recognising the necessity of staying competitive in a rapidly changing global economy, ASEAN has implemented measures to protect intellectual property rights (IPR) and enhance financial integration through frameworks like the ASEAN Banking Integration Framework (ABIF). The ABIF allows banks that meet stringent financial stability and regulatory compliance standards, known as Qualified ASEAN Banks (QABs), to operate more freely across member states through bilateral agreements, addressing differences in readiness and market access. Together, these efforts are crucial for promoting financial stability and supporting regional economic growth, particularly as digital transformation accelerates. Initiatives to develop human capital through skill-building and education further support the growth of innovative industries. ASEAN's commitment to inclusive business practices ensures that economic progress benefits all segments of society, promoting sustainable and equitable development across member states.

The third characteristic, enhanced connectivity and sectoral cooperation, underscores the importance of physical and institutional connectivity. ASEAN has recognised that improved transport, energy, and digital infrastructure connectivity is vital for integrating the region and facilitating trade and investment. For instance, the Master Plan on ASEAN Connectivity 2025 (MPAC 2025) serves as a key framework for building regional transport links, improving supply chain efficiency, and fostering digital connectivity. This initiative extends to developing "smart cities" through the ASEAN Smart Cities Network (ASCN), integrating sustainable urbanisation with modern technologies to meet the needs of the region's rapidly growing population. The development of smart cities, especially in areas such as digital infrastructure and sustainable urban planning, is central to ASEAN's vision of a connected and efficient region.

The fourth characteristic, resilient, inclusive, people-oriented, and people-centred ASEAN, emerged in response to the COVID-19 pandemic, highlighting the necessity for resilience in economic and social systems. During the pandemic, intra-ASEAN trade was crucial in ensuring the continuous supply of essential goods, including medical supplies and food, helping member states manage disruptions in global supply chains. The growth in intra-ASEAN trade demonstrated the region's resilience and adaptability to global shocks, reinforcing the importance of building a people-centred and inclusive community. ASEAN's initiatives to build resilience also encompass social and environmental dimensions, such as social protection, climate change adaptation, and disaster risk reduction, promoting sustainable livelihoods for its diverse population.

The final characteristic, global ASEAN, embodies ASEAN's strategy to remain actively engaged with the global economy. The signing of the Regional Comprehensive Economic Partnership (RCEP) in 2020 is one of ASEAN's most significant achievements. As the world's largest trade agreement, RCEP brings together ASEAN's ten member states and five dialogue partners: China, Japan, South Korea, Australia, and New Zealand. This agreement encompasses a market of approximately 2.2 billion people—about 30% of the global population—and accounts for around 30% of global GDP, equating to roughly $28.2 trillion (based on 2019 figures) and 28.8% of international trade.

The RCEP's comprehensive framework eliminates tariffs, streamlines customs procedures, and facilitates investments across member economies. It is expected to deepen ASEAN's economic integration. The RCEP is projected to contribute significantly to the global economy, adding approximately $245 billion in real income annually by 2030, according to the Asian Development Bank (ADB). This translates into a potential annual GDP boost of 0.6% for ASEAN member states, highlighting the agreement's critical role in fostering economic growth and creating 2.8 million jobs. RCEP builds upon ASEAN's existing network of free trade agreements with its dialogue partners, streamlining trade and investment flows across the region. By enhancing market access and regional connectivity, RCEP reinforces ASEAN's position as a dynamic player in the global economic landscape, ensuring its continued relevance in shaping international trade and economic policies.

In essence, the AEC Blueprint 2025 positions ASEAN to achieve even deeper economic integration, foster resilience against external shocks, and ensure sustainable growth. ASEAN continues to drive its agenda toward creating a more integrated, dynamic, and inclusive economic community by focusing on trade liberalisation, enhancing connectivity, promoting innovation, and engaging with global partners.

Significance of the Master Plan on Connectivity

In order to address the challenges of bridging gaps in regional infrastructure, enhancing trade efficiency, and supporting economic growth, ASEAN introduced the Master Plan on ASEAN Connectivity 2015 (MPAC 2015). The MPAC 2015 (2009–2015) aimed to balance connectivity across mainland and maritime ASEAN, addressing the diverse needs of its member states. As part of this plan to develop infrastructure for mainland countries to boost cross-border land transport and trade, the ASEAN Highway Network (AHN) aimed to connect key economic corridors across countries like Thailand, Myanmar, Vietnam, and Laos through upgraded roads, reducing trade barriers and improving transportation efficiency.

The Singapore-Kunming Rail Link (SKRL) was another major initiative to establish a seamless rail connection from Singapore to China, passing through mainland countries like Malaysia and Thailand. Moreover, enhancing the navigability of the Mekong River and developing river ports improved trade routes and regional connectivity, allowing efficient movement of goods and economic integration among mainland countries.

For maritime ASEAN, which includes archipelagic nations like Indonesia, the Philippines, and Brunei, MPAC focused on enhancing sea transport and inter-island connectivity. Developing short-sea shipping and roll-on/roll-off (RoRo) networks was central to these efforts, aiming to reduce transportation costs and connect remote islands more effectively to regional markets. Port upgrades were also crucial, with major ports in Indonesia, Malaysia, and the Philippines earmarked for expansion to handle larger cargo volumes and reduce congestion, effectively turning these ports into regional trade hubs. The proposed ASEAN Single Shipping Market aimed to harmonise regulations for shipping services, streamline customs processes, and create a competitive maritime environment across the region.

Balancing projects for mainland and maritime ASEAN ensured that all member states benefited from the region's connectivity initiatives regardless of geography. By addressing the infrastructure needs of land and sea transport, MPAC contributed to an integrated ASEAN, supporting economic growth, reducing trade costs, and fostering regional unity. Building on this foundation, the MPAC 2025 was developed to deepen connectivity efforts further and respond to emerging regional challenges. MPAC 2025 focuses on five strategic areas: sustainable infrastructure, digital innovation, seamless logistics, regulatory excellence, and people mobility. Recognising the rapid technological advances and the need for sustainable development, MPAC 2025 emphasises infrastructure modernisation, enhancing digital connectivity, and promoting regulatory coherence across borders.

In mainland ASEAN, the focus shifted towards sustainable transport networks, developing green infrastructure, and enhancing smart city connectivity to improve urban mobility. For maritime ASEAN, MPAC 2025 continues to support projects to enhance port infrastructure and inter-island connectivity but with a stronger emphasis on integrating digital technology to streamline logistics and facilitate smoother trade flows. The plan also emphasises digital innovation to improve cross-border e-commerce, digital financial services, and cyber connectivity across mainland and maritime ASEAN countries. Through MPAC 2025, ASEAN aims to achieve a higher level of regional integration by enhancing connectivity in a way that supports sustainable economic development, enables technological advancement, and promotes the free movement of people and goods, strengthening the ASEAN Community and its role on the global stage.

Behind the scenes on the MPAC development

Setting aside the benefits of MPAC, if I am to recall the making of this plan, I distinctly remember it being far from easy. The ASEAN Secretariat team faced a significant challenge in developing the MPAC 2015. The first draft was imbalanced, focusing heavily on connectivity across the mainland of ASEAN and less on maritime nations like Indonesia and the Philippines. It was also perceived that the CLMV countries—Cambodia, Laos, Myanmar, and Vietnam—stood to benefit more than others, given their greater need for infrastructural development. This imbalance naturally led to concerns from the maritime members, who felt that the plan did not adequately address their unique connectivity needs.

As the Principal Director of the Bureau of Economic Integration and Finance, I led my team through a recalibration process. Our goal was to develop a balanced document that all ASEAN member states would embrace. We understood that the CLMV countries needed robust connectivity for growth and to bridge the economic disparities between the region's members. However, it was equally important to address the concerns of the maritime ASEAN members, who sought better integration within the regional framework.

The rationale for focusing more on maritime connectivity was clear. A large part of ASEAN's population resides in archipelagic nations, making efficient sea transport and port infrastructure crucial for their economic development. In countries like Indonesia and the Philippines, which comprise thousands of islands, maritime transport is often the only means of connecting remote areas to major markets. Improving maritime connectivity—by enhancing ports, creating efficient shipping routes, and developing inter-island RoRo networks—was essential for lowering transportation costs, reducing transit times, and boosting trade. Without it, the archipelagic nations risked being left out of the growth trajectory that the mainland countries might experience through better land-based connectivity.

Furthermore, developing maritime routes would help integrate Southeast Asia's maritime and mainland supply chains, improving trade efficiency and the movement of goods across the region. Maritime connectivity is inherently important not just for the growth of archipelagic nations but also for the broader economic resilience of the region. Strengthening maritime links allows all ASEAN member states to access international markets more effectively, promotes greater intraregional trade, and contributes to regional economic stability by ensuring that transport networks are diversified and adaptable.

Balancing mainland and maritime connectivity was also critical because pockets of underdevelopment existed not only in the CLMV countries but also within some of ASEAN's founding members. Indonesia, for instance, faces significant development gaps between its eastern and western regions, and the Philippines has areas that are disconnected from the main economic hubs. Ensuring that all ASEAN countries, including the founding members, could benefit from enhanced connectivity was vital for achieving equitable development and social cohesion across the region. Without addressing these disparities, the economic integration envisioned under the AEC Blueprint risked leaving certain regions and populations behind, undermining the inclusive growth goal.

To address this, we ensured that projects aimed at improving maritime infrastructure, such as enhancing port facilities and developing short-sea shipping and

RoRo networks, were included as key strategies. The benefits of these initiatives went beyond the archipelagic nations and aimed at strengthening the overall regional supply chain, making intra-ASEAN transport and trade more efficient. Creating a stronger maritime connectivity framework meant improving access to essential services, supporting tourism, and encouraging greater people-to-people connectivity—key components in building an integrated ASEAN community.

By the time the ASEAN Heads of Government adopted the MPAC, it featured a more comprehensive approach that acknowledged the importance of mainland and maritime connectivity. This focus supported the development of archipelagic countries and ensured that the overarching goal of building a well-connected, competitive, and resilient ASEAN was achieved for all member states. Addressing the varying needs of both mainland and maritime ASEAN and ensuring that benefits reached all members played a crucial role in making the region more economically balanced, integrated, and inclusive.

ASEAN Single Window

The ASEAN Single Window (ASW) is a key initiative under the AEC that streamlines customs procedures by allowing the electronic exchange of documents between ASEAN member states. Operational since 2018, it has significantly reduced the time and cost of cross-border trade by simplifying customs clearance.

The ASW enables real-time electronic data exchange, facilitating faster clearance of goods and improving transparency. It has been especially valuable during the pandemic, ensuring that essential goods could be processed and moved across borders without delays. Its role in reducing paperwork and eliminating bottlenecks has made it a vital component of ASEAN's push to create a single market and production base.

The ASW has significantly enhanced trade efficiency within the ASEAN region. By September 2023, ASEAN member states had exchanged approximately 4.4 million digital customs forms through the ASW, substantially increasing from about 137,230 forms in late 2018. This digital platform has saved traders an estimated $2,300 per transaction between 2018 and 2022, totalling approximately $6.5 billion in savings. The ASW's implementation has been pivotal in advancing the ASEAN Economic Community's seamless trade and economic integration goal.

ASEAN external economic relations

ASEAN's extensive network of Free Trade Agreements is one of its greatest strengths in connecting with the global economy. These agreements have facilitated greater market access for ASEAN exports, attracted investment, and driven regional growth, shaping the economic landscape across Southeast Asia.

The **ASEAN-China Free Trade Agreement (ACFTA),** signed in 2002, has played a crucial role in enhancing economic ties, making China ASEAN's largest trading partner. By 2022, trade between ASEAN and China reached an impressive $722 billion, accounting for around 18.8% of ASEAN's total trade. This growth underscores China's importance as a key economic partner for ASEAN. The ACFTA has facilitated tariff elimination, enhanced trade in services, and encouraged investment flows between the two regions. It has bolstered economic exchanges and fostered broader connectivity and supply chain linkages, deepening the ASEAN-China partnership.

Another cornerstone of ASEAN's economic integration efforts is the **ASEAN-Japan Comprehensive Economic Partnership (AJCEP)**, signed in 2008. By 2022, trade between ASEAN and Japan has reached approximately $268 billion, reflecting the depth of engagement between these regions. Japan continues to be a major investor in ASEAN, with FDI exceeding $27 billion in 2022. The AJCEP has been instrumental in promoting trade liberalisation, investment cooperation, and economic collaboration across critical sectors such as technology, infrastructure, and energy, reinforcing economic integration and enhancing regional supply chain connectivity.

The **ASEAN-Korea Free Trade Agreement (AKFTA)**, effective since 2006, has facilitated robust trade and investment between ASEAN and South Korea, particularly in technology, manufacturing, services, and agriculture. By 2022, bilateral trade reached approximately $222 billion, showcasing the growing economic ties between the two regions. South Korea's investment in ASEAN has also been significant, with over $12 billion in FDI recorded in 2022. The AKFTA includes provisions for tariff reduction, trade facilitation, and investment promotion, fostering deeper supply chain linkages and broader economic cooperation, which has significantly contributed to ASEAN's economic resilience.

The **ASEAN-India Free Trade Agreement (AIFTA)**, signed in 2010, has greatly strengthened trade, services, and investment relations between ASEAN and India. By 2022, trade between the two regions reached an estimated $113 billion, reflecting a solid economic partnership. AIFTA focuses on tariff reductions, services liberalisation, and investment facilitation, expanding market access and developing commercial linkages, particularly in sectors like information technology, pharmaceuticals, textiles, and agribusiness. This supports economic growth in both regions.

Similarly, the **ASEAN-Australia-New Zealand Free Trade Area (AANZFTA)**, signed in 2010, has enhanced trade, investment, and economic cooperation across ASEAN, Australia, and New Zealand. By 2022, two-way trade among them stood at around $116 billion. This agreement encompasses various sectors, including goods, services, and investment, with provisions to reduce tariffs, enhance trade facilitation, and improve market access for businesses, thereby strengthening economic integration among the three regions.

These trade agreements have collectively contributed to ASEAN's economic growth, leading to deeper regional and global integration. The combined impact of these agreements has positioned ASEAN as a central economic hub in the Asia-Pacific region, enhancing its role in international trade and investment networks. The FTAs are critical for ensuring ASEAN's integration into the global economy while providing its members access to new markets and investment opportunities. Notably, the FTAs, including the RCEP, have significantly boosted the region's trade.

One critical aspect is that while pursuing external economic relations and FTAs, ASEAN has remained committed to its core principles of consensus, non-interference, and respect for sovereignty. These principles have guided ASEAN's approach to regional economic integration and engagement with global partners. In negotiating its FTAs, ASEAN has aimed to ensure that the agreements promote mutual benefits while preserving the autonomy of member states and the region's collective unity. The emphasis on these principles has been particularly important in cases where economic discussions intersect with political and social considerations. This reflects ASEAN's commitment to balancing economic openness with maintaining its foundational values and regional coherence. This approach has been pivotal in ensuring that trade agreements serve the interests of all ASEAN members while reinforcing the Association's centrality and role in regional diplomacy and global trade.

ASEAN-European Union FTA talks: a test of unity

The negotiations for an ASEAN-European Union FTA were launched in 2007. As the Principal Director of the Bureau of Economic Integration and Finance and subsequently, as the Deputy Secretary General of the ASEAN Economic Community (DSG AEC) in 2009, I led the Secretariat delegation in discussions between ASEAN senior economic officials and European Commission officials to advance our discussion of a potential free trade agreement between our two regions.

Both ASEAN and the European Union were keen on establishing deeper economic ties, and hopes were high that the negotiations could pave the way for a significant partnership. However, things quickly became complicated. As part of its standard practice, the European Union insisted on signing a partnership and cooperation agreement (PCA) with provisions such as a commitment to human rights, democracy, and the rule of law. This demand from the European Union was more than a routine requirement for ASEAN in FTA negotiations. As we sat across from the European Union delegation during the meeting, it became clear that this PCA was more than a broad statement on, among others, democratic values. The proposed conditions were seen as directly targeting Myanmar, then a member of ASEAN with a contentious political situation. The European Union, driven by the strong voices of some of its members, was vocal about Myanmar's internal issues, making it evident that the FTA could not proceed without addressing this point. On the other hand, ASEAN wanted a region-to-region FTA that would include all its members.

This situation posed a major challenge for ASEAN members. The ASEAN Charter was grounded in the principles of non-interference, sovereignty, and consensus—values that were non-negotiable for our regional unity. Accepting the European Union's condition would set a precedent, infringing upon the internal affairs of member states and exposing ASEAN to external political scrutiny. It would compromise ASEAN's consensus-driven nature and risk dividing the unity we had worked so hard to build.

I recall luridly the tension in the room. As part of the Secretariat team, we rallied around our member states to present a unified stance. The European Union delegation pushed hard, emphasising the importance of human rights as part of any of their trade agreements. But we knew this was more than just about Myanmar. The stakes were about protecting ASEAN's principles and sovereignty and ensuring that no single member would be put in a position of political isolation.

The ASEAN delegation diplomatically rejected the need for a precursor political document and the conditions tied to it. The message was clear. While ASEAN was committed to developing economic partnerships, it would not do so at the expense of its principles of unity and non-interference. The EU's insistence on a political clause became a roadblock that prevented a region-wide FTA, and the talks did not move forward as both sides hoped. Besides, the diverse economic landscapes, varying development levels among ASEAN member states, and the lack of technical expertise and resources to engage in complex trade negotiations with the EU made it difficult to negotiate a region-to-region FTA.

However, this did not mark the end of ASEAN-European Union trade relations. Recognising the stalemate, the EU shifted its strategy, moving away from a region-to-region approach and focusing instead on bilateral FTAs with individual ASEAN countries. Over the next two decades, ASEAN countries, like Singapore and Vietnam, successfully negotiated their FTAs with the European Union that came into force in 2019 and 2020, respectively. These agreements set a precedent for economic cooperation between the European Union and individual ASEAN members, with negotiations continuing with countries like Thailand, the Philippines, and Indonesia.

The 1990s negotiations were a watershed moment in ASEAN's foreign economic ties. They demonstrated the organisation's resolve to stand together as a single entity and reaffirmed its sovereignty, consensus, and non-interference values. The experience showed the tricky combination of developing foreign partnerships and negotiating free trade agreements while maintaining

ASEAN's identity and principles. It highlighted the power of unity in the face of external pressures.

Since then, ASEAN and the European Union re-initiated formal talks on a Free Trade Agreement (FTA) in 2017 by establishing a working group; however, progress has been limited. One of the primary challenges stems from the varying capacities and ambitions among ASEAN member states, which complicates negotiations. Besides, rising protectionism in both regions poses further obstacles to achieving a comprehensive agreement. The two regions' differing environmental, social, and governance priorities will increasingly become focal points in trade negotiations. While the potential benefits of an FTA are significant for both parties, the path forward could be more complex. Therefore, pursuing bilateral FTAs among individual ASEAN member states and the European Union may be a more viable approach before a region-to-region FTA can be realised. This incremental strategy could help build trust and address specific concerns before committing to a broader agreement.

Financial cooperation

ASEAN has made significant strides in advancing financial cooperation to promote economic stability and regional integration. Initiatives like the ASEAN Financial Integration Framework (AFIF) and the ASEAN Banking Integration Framework (ABIF) are critical in enhancing cross-border banking, capital markets, and financial services. The AFIF provides a comprehensive roadmap for harmonising financial policies and regulations across member states, fostering a resilient and integrated financial system that supports regional economic development.

The ABIF, as a key pillar of AFIF, focuses specifically on enabling Qualified ASEAN Banks (QABs) to operate seamlessly across borders, promoting competition, financial inclusion, and deeper economic linkages within ASEAN. These frameworks allow for greater capital flows, regulatory harmonisation, and financial stability, facilitating smoother financial transactions across member states. Furthermore, ASEAN has been working towards integrating payment systems through the ASEAN Payment Connectivity initiative, enabling real-time cross-border transactions to enhance regional trade and investment by reducing transaction costs and improving financial inclusion.

A key component of ASEAN's financial safety net is the Chiang Mai Initiative Multilateralisation (CMIM), established in response to the 1997 Asian Financial Crisis to provide liquidity support to APT members (ASEAN, China, Japan, and South Korea) during financial distress. As of 2022, the CMIM has a fund pool of $240 billion, acting as a safeguard to ensure that member states have access to emergency funds, thereby enhancing economic resilience. In addition to the CMIM, the ASEAN+3 Macroeconomic Research Office (AMRO) based in Singapore has a crucial role in monitoring regional economies and providing policy advice, ensuring that member states are equipped with the necessary information to steer financial challenges effectively. On the other hand, efforts to develop a more integrated capital market are led by the ASEAN Capital Markets Forum (ACMF), which promotes regulatory harmonisation, transparency, and investor protection. Through the ACMF, ASEAN aims to create a seamless capital market that attracts global investors and supports sustainable economic growth within the region.

Challenges and opportunities

While ASEAN has made substantial progress in integrating its economies under the AEC framework, several challenges hinder its full economic potential. One of the primary challenges is the presence of non-tariff barriers (NTBs) and regulatory fragmentation across member states. Despite reducing tariffs, NTBs like complex customs procedures, inconsistent standards, licensing requirements, and import restrictions continue to limit the free flow of goods, services, and investments. This affects intra-ASEAN trade and makes it difficult for businesses to access regional markets seamlessly. Progress on NTB reduction has been uneven, with certain industries, such as agriculture, automotive, and services, still facing significant barriers.

Another challenge lies in the digital divide among ASEAN member states. While Singapore, Malaysia, and Thailand are at the forefront of digital transformation, less developed countries like Cambodia, Laos, Myanmar, and

Vietnam face challenges regarding digital infrastructure, internet penetration, and technical capabilities. This digital disparity poses obstacles to realising ASEAN's vision of becoming a digitally connected and inclusive economy. For example, according to a 2021 World Bank report, internet penetration rates vary significantly across ASEAN, ranging from over 88% in Singapore to around 30-40% in Myanmar and Laos, impacting the growth of e-commerce and digital services.

Despite these challenges, the AEC Blueprint 2025 provides a roadmap for deepening integration and tapping into new economic opportunities. One such opportunity is the potential for ASEAN to capitalise on the digital economy. With a combined digital economy market projected to exceed $330 billion by 2025, initiatives like the ASEAN Digital Integration Framework aim to reduce digital trade barriers, foster cross-border e-commerce, and improve cybersecurity.

One critical opportunity is the development of the ASEAN Smart Cities Network (ASCN). Twenty-six pilot cities across ASEAN are working towards sustainable urban solutions, leveraging smart technologies for infrastructure development, waste management, and transportation. Furthermore, signing the RCEP in 2020 presents ASEAN with a path for greater economic integration and competitiveness. As the world's largest trade arrangement, the RCEP offers opportunities to diversify supply chains, attract FDI, and integrate into global value chains.

Lastly, the rise of green technologies and the focus on sustainable development provide ASEAN with avenues to build resilient economies. Initiatives like the ASEAN Green Recovery Framework emphasise investments in renewable energy, sustainable agriculture, and environmentally friendly technologies, aiming to achieve the United Nations Sustainable Development Goals (SDGs) while fostering economic growth.

In essence, the AEC has emerged as a pivotal force driving ASEAN's economic success, promoting deeper integration and enhancing its global competitiveness. The AEC Blueprint 2025 builds on these achievements by improving regional connectivity, fostering innovation, and ensuring resilience in the face of future challenges. Intra-ASEAN trade has proven vital, especially during the COVID-19 pandemic, as it played a crucial role in maintaining supply chain continuity and economic stability across the region. The significant rebound in intra-ASEAN trade—growing to $710 billion in 2021—demonstrates the region's capacity to adapt and thrive amidst global disruptions. Besides, with the ongoing implementation of initiatives like the ASW, which streamlines customs procedures and enhances trade efficiency, and the robust framework of FTAs that connect ASEAN with key global partners, the region is strategically positioned to achieve its vision of becoming a highly integrated and dynamic economic community.

As ASEAN continues to traverse the complexities of the global economy, its commitment to fostering inclusivity and resilience will be essential for sustainable growth. This will ensure that the benefits of integration are shared among all member states and the people.

> *"Economic stability and growth are essential components of peace. Through the ASEAN Economic Community, member states have created a robust framework for economic integration, ensuring that prosperity becomes a common goal, reinforcing stability across the region."*
>
> **Pushpanathan Sundram, Author**

Chapter 5

Political & Security Cooperation – The ASEAN Political-Security Community

"The ASEAN Political-Security Community has its genesis of over four decades of close co-operation and solidarity. The ASEAN Heads of States/Governments, at their Summit in Kuala Lumpur in December 1997 envisioned a concert of Southeast Asian nations, outward looking, living in peace, stability and prosperity, bonded together in partnership in dynamic development and in a community of caring societies."

ASEAN Political-Security Community Blueprint, ASEAN Secretariat, June 2009

One of ASEAN's most remarkable achievements lies in its unwavering commitment to fostering peace, stability, and security across Southeast Asia. With the establishment of the ASEAN Political Security Community (APSC), ASEAN has taken a proactive stance in addressing regional security challenges, promoting political cooperation, and ensuring that disputes are resolved peacefully through dialogue and diplomacy. This is not just a theoretical framework; it's about creating a safe and stable environment for the 680 million people living in this vibrant region. The APSC stands as one of the three pillars of the ASEAN Community, alongside the AEC and ASCC. This integration reflects ASEAN's dedication to fostering a politically cohesive and secure Southeast Asia, where member states collaboratively tackle traditional and non-traditional security threats.

In this chapter, we will journey through the evolution of the APSC, exploring its key mechanisms and the initiatives ASEAN has undertaken to promote political cooperation, conflict resolution, and regional security. You will discover how ASEAN addresses pressing transnational issues like terrorism, piracy, and cybersecurity and its efforts to build trust among regional powers through platforms like the ARF. This is not just about policies and strategies; it's about the real impacts on people's lives in the region and the collective efforts to create a safer Southeast Asia for everyone.

The formation of APSC

The idea of creating an APSC was first articulated in the Bali Concord II of 2003, where ASEAN leaders outlined a vision for a more politically integrated and secure region. The goal was to create an environment where member states could work together to address traditional security challenges, such as territorial disputes and non-traditional threats, like transnational crime and terrorism.

The APSC was formally established as part of the ASEAN Charter in 2007, aiming to position ASEAN as a key player in maintaining peace and security within Southeast Asia. To guide this vision, the APSC Blueprint 2015 and successor Blueprint 2025 lay a comprehensive roadmap for deepening political and security cooperation among member states. The Blueprint 2025 seek to build a rules-based community that upholds the principles of the rule of law, good governance, and respect for human rights, ensuring transparent and accountable institutions across the region.

It also aspires to create a cohesive and peaceful ASEAN, where disputes are resolved amicably through dialogue and diplomacy, fostering an environment of trust and cooperation. The APSC emphasises the need to develop a resilient community capable of effectively addressing non-traditional security challenges, such as terrorism, human trafficking, and health crises like pandemics, through regional collaboration and robust mechanisms for prevention, response, and recovery. Its overarching goal is to create a region where the security of each member state is tied to the region's security as a whole: regional resilience buttresses national resilience and vice versa.

Core principles of APSC

The APSC is anchored in core principles that formalise ASEAN's approach to political and security cooperation, fostering peace and stability across Southeast Asia. Non-interference in the internal affairs of member states is a foundational principle, historically preventing regional conflicts from arising out of political differences. While this principle has contributed significantly to stability, it also presents challenges when ASEAN needs to address sensitive issues like human rights violations or internal political crises. Balancing non-interference with the promotion of good governance, human rights, and the rule of law has become part of ASEAN's evolving strategy, reflecting its commitment to regional harmony alongside recognising emerging security concerns.

The APSC is guided by ASEAN's consensus-based decision-making process, ensuring that all members collectively agree on regional policies. This approach has helped maintain unity, fostering trust and collaboration among member states. However, the consensus model can also slow decision-making, presenting a challenge when quick responses to emerging security threats are required. Nevertheless, it has proven crucial in avoiding conflict and nurturing cooperative relationships within ASEAN.

Another key principle is the commitment to peaceful conflict resolution through dialogue and diplomacy. The Treaty of Amity and Cooperation (TAC) of 1976 is the cornerstone of this approach, enshrining the values of mutual respect, non-use of force, and peaceful settlement of disputes. These principles have been pivotal in maintaining regional peace and fostering a collaborative environment. The APSC builds on these foundational principles by developing conflict prevention, management, and resolution mechanisms. It incorporates early warning systems to anticipate potential conflicts, confidence-building measures to promote trust among member states, and preventive diplomacy to address disputes before they escalate. These mechanisms reflect the APSC's broader goal of maintaining regional stability through dialogue, cooperation, and a rules-based framework.

One challenge frequently faced when drafting ASEAN documents was balancing the different governance systems of member states. Democracy was a term that carried weight, reflecting ideals of participation, freedom, and rights. However, it was not a universally accepted concept in practice within the region. Some member states fully embraced democracy, while others followed different political paths, potentially divisive the term.

Throughout the early years of drafting major ASEAN documents, the word "democracy" remained a sensitive issue. I recall many extensive discussions about whether the term should be used and, if so, how it should be framed. It was clear that ASEAN needed to project an image of inclusiveness and participation. Still, at the same time, it could not impose a singular model of governance that did not align with the political realities of all its member states. The challenge was to find terminology that respected the diverse governance systems across Southeast Asia while still upholding ASEAN's vision for a community rooted in shared values.

The solution came in the form of a compromise: the phrase "all sectors of society." This phrase became a flexible alternative to describe "democracy," carrying the spirit of inclusivity and participation without being explicitly prescriptive about the form of governance. It appeared in critical documents like the ASEAN Charter and the APSC Blueprint 2025. Including "democracy" and "all sectors of society" in these documents was a delicate balance—a reflection of ASEAN's principle of consensus and respect for sovereignty.

The Charter, which formalised ASEAN's legal status and established its guiding principles, was a turning point. For the first time, "democracy" was formally included in ASEAN's core principles, but it was accompanied by the more inclusive "all sectors of society." This language choice signalled that while ASEAN aspired to democratic principles, it remained open to varied forms of participation that respected each country's governance. The pattern was the same in the APSC Blueprint 2025. "Democracy" was recognised as a value, while "all sectors of society" ensured that participation extended beyond the political elite, embracing the full spectrum of communities within ASEAN countries. This dual approach demonstrated ASEAN's pragmatism—finding a middle ground accommodating diverse governance systems while promoting unity and inclusiveness.

Reflecting on this compromise, it's clear that ASEAN's strength lies in its ability to craft language that reflects both aspiration and reality. The use of "all sectors of society" alongside "democracy" in these foundational documents is a testament to ASEAN's commitment to building a cohesive and inclusive regional community, one that respects diversity while promoting shared values.

Key mechanisms of APSC

The APSC operates through various mechanisms to address traditional and non-traditional security challenges, foster regional cooperation, and enhance trust among ASEAN member states. Key among these mechanisms is the ASEAN Regional Forum (ARF), established in 1994 as Southeast Asia's most inclusive platform for security dialogue.

The ARF brings together ASEAN members and 27 external partners, including major powers such as the United States, China, Japan, and Russia, to address pressing security issues. With its focus on Confidence-Building Measures (CBMs) and preventive diplomacy, the ARF has facilitated frameworks like the ARF Work Plan on Counter-Terrorism and Transnational Crime. This framework enhances intelligence-sharing and regional coordination on issues such as human trafficking and terrorism financing. The ARF has also played a critical role in engaging North Korea in nuclear disarmament discussions, providing a unique channel for dialogue.

Another significant mechanism is the ASEAN Defence Ministers' Meeting (ADMM), established in 2006 as the primary platform for defence cooperation within ASEAN. The ADMM enables member states to address pressing security challenges collaboratively with initiatives like the ASEAN Direct Communications Infrastructure (ADI), a crisis hotline that has been operational since 2014. This hotline was successfully tested during the 2018 disaster simulation exercises, underscoring its reliability for rapid emergency communication.

Expanding this cooperation, the ADMM-Plus, formed in 2010, includes dialogue partners such as China, the United States, and India, focusing on areas such as counterterrorism, maritime security, and humanitarian assistance. The 2019 Maritime Security Exercise in Singapore and the South China Sea demonstrated the ADMM-Plus's practical contributions, including joint patrols to combat piracy and illegal fishing. The ASEAN Peacekeeping Centres Network (APCN), operational since 2011, further complements these efforts by preparing military personnel for joint missions, enhancing the region's peacekeeping and disaster management capabilities.

The ASEAN Intergovernmental Commission on Human Rights (AICHR), established in 2009, is another cornerstone of the APSC. Despite its limited enforcement powers, AICHR has been instrumental in integrating human rights into ASEAN's policy framework. Its collaboration with civil society organisations has resulted in initiatives like the ASEAN Enabling Masterplan 2025, which focuses on disability rights and has led to improvements in accessibility in Thailand and Vietnam. The commission also plays a vital role in facilitating discussions on sensitive issues such as migrant workers' rights.

While these mechanisms form the core of the APSC, the ASEAN Institute for Peace and Reconciliation (AIPR) is a supportive mechanism for promoting conflict resolution, peacebuilding, and reconciliation in the region. Operational since 2012, the AIPR has conducted research and capacity-building programs to address intra-state and inter-state conflicts. The AIPR's focus on gender inclusion in peacebuilding has further strengthened ASEAN's capacity to address conflict through innovative and inclusive approaches. It has done this through initiatives such as the ASEAN Women for Peace Registry (AWPR) and training programs aligned with the UN's Women, Peace, and Security (WPS) Agenda, enhancing ASEAN's capacity for inclusive conflict resolution.

Contribution of external partners in APSC

External partners are pivotal in supporting the APSC objectives. Through platforms such as the ARF and the ADMM-Plus, ASEAN collaborates with major powers to address regional security challenges effectively. These partnerships are essential in areas such as counterterrorism, maritime security, and disaster relief, contributing significantly to regional stability, resilience, and peacebuilding.

For example, the United States' security cooperation has been a cornerstone of ASEAN's engagement with external partners. The United States actively supports ASEAN's security agenda through its robust participation in the ADMM-Plus and the ARF. It provides military assistance, technical and strategic intelligence sharing, and capacity-building programs to enhance ASEAN member states' counterterrorism capabilities and improve maritime security operations. Moreover, its support extends to humanitarian assistance and disaster relief, helping to build ASEAN's capacity to respond effectively to natural disasters. It also promotes principles of a free and open Indo-Pacific, encouraging rules-based regional security cooperation.

Similarly, China's role in regional security has grown substantially in recent years, as China has actively sought to engage ASEAN in multiple security areas. Although there are strategic complexities in the region, especially concerning the South China Sea, it has become a crucial partner in addressing non-traditional security threats like counterterrorism, disaster relief, and public health cooperation. Platforms such as the ARF provide a space for ASEAN and China to deepen dialogue on key security issues, fostering an environment of mutual trust. Its involvement in pandemic preparedness, such as during the COVID-19 crisis, has emphasised its commitment to supporting ASEAN's capacity to respond to public health emergencies. Furthermore, various cooperative agreements have contributed to strengthening emergency response mechanisms and enhancing regional peace and resilience.

Japan, too, remains central to ASEAN's efforts to maintain maritime safety and security at sea. It has been one of ASEAN's most reliable and consistent partners in promoting maritime security. Through initiatives like the ASEAN-Japan Maritime Cooperation, Japan provides technical assistance, capacity-building programs, and financial support that enhances ASEAN's ability to safeguard its maritime borders and combat transnational crimes, such as piracy and smuggling. Japan's contributions to capacity-building extend to training programs, the supply of patrol vessels, and technology transfer, bolstering the maritime capabilities of ASEAN member states. Japan's approach to maritime security also emphasises freedom of navigation, the rule of law, and peaceful dispute resolution, principles that align closely with ASEAN's priorities.

These partnerships with external powers help ASEAN address complex security challenges, enhance regional capacity in traditional and non-traditional security areas, and uphold the region's stability and development. Cooperation with the United States, China, Japan, and other partners through mechanisms like the ARF and ADMM-Plus underscores ASEAN's strategy of engaging external powers constructively while preserving its centrality in the regional security architecture.

Challenges to political and security cooperation

The APSC faces numerous challenges in fostering a stable and secure Southeast Asia. While progress has been made, the region's geopolitical dynamics and internal complexities continue to pose significant hurdles. Territorial disputes in the South China Sea remain a critical concern, with China's assertive claims and activities, such as the militarisation of artificial islands and the imposition of unilateral fishing bans, raising tensions with several ASEAN member states.

Efforts by ASEAN to manage these disputes through diplomacy and dialogue led to the 2002 Declaration on the Conduct of Parties in the South China SEA (DOC), which called for peaceful dispute resolution and confidence-building measures. However, the development of a legally binding Code of Conduct in the South China Sea (COC) has been protracted, with ongoing negotiations facing delays due to geopolitical complexities and the challenge of reaching a consensus among all parties. These dynamics highlight the delicate balance ASEAN must maintain to promote maritime stability, uphold international law such as the United Nations Convention on the Law of the Sea (UNCLOS), and preserve its role in regional security management.

Human rights and governance remain another challenge for the APSC, as ASEAN's principle of non-interference often limits its ability to address human rights issues within member states. The organisation has made efforts to promote good governance, the rule of law, and respect for human rights through initiatives like the ASEAN Human Rights Declaration (AHRD) and the establishment of the AICHR. However, the AICHR's advisory nature and the absence of enforcement mechanisms have constrained its ability to address violations effectively.

ASEAN's consensus-based decision-making process, which prioritises regional stability and cohesion over public condemnation or intervention, further complicates the promotion of human rights. This creates a tension between adhering to ASEAN's foundational principles of non-interference and sovereignty and the aspiration to uphold human rights and governance standards, which remains a delicate balancing act for the APSC.

Coordination among ASEAN member states presents a substantial problem. The region's different political systems, which range from democracies to monarchies and one-party regimes, result in disparities in governance structures and security goals, which can inhibit effective policy execution. While the APSC has made strides in political growth, dispute resolution, and common security norms, conflicting state interests and attitudes to sovereignty frequently hamper policy alignment. The emphasis on consensus-based decision-making can hinder policy implementation or lead to lowest-common-denominator agreements that do not adequately address critical security problems. Responses to diverse security concerns, such as counterterrorism, maritime disputes, and cybersecurity threats, can differ significantly among member nations, limiting ASEAN's capacity to implement cohesive actions or plans. Disparities in economic growth and institutional capacities impede harmonised security measures, with less developed members having a more difficult time attaining APSC objectives.

Moreover, the region grapples with rising nontraditional security threats that require coordinated regional responses. Climate change, transnational crime, cyber threats, and public health emergencies have emerged as critical concerns that transcend national borders. The COVID-19 pandemic exposed the gaps in ASEAN's public health infrastructure and cross-border coordination, highlighting the need for stronger health security mechanisms.

Meanwhile, cybersecurity is an emerging challenge, with increasing incidents of cyberattacks on critical infrastructure, businesses, and financial systems across Southeast Asia. Though ASEAN has introduced various frameworks to address these non-traditional threats, including the ASEAN Digital Economy Framework Agreement, ASEAN Plan of Action on Mitigating Transboundary Haze Pollution, and the ASEAN Agreement on Disaster Management and Emergency Response (AADMER), the diverse capacities and priorities among member states result in fragmented responses and hinder comprehensive solutions.

Balancing relations with major powers has become an increasingly complex aspect of ASEAN's role in the regional security landscape. ASEAN's centrality in the region allows it to act as a bridge between competing powers, particularly the United States and China. However, this balancing act has become more complex as geopolitical contestation intensifies. While both the United States and China are critical economic and security partners for ASEAN, their strategic interests in the Indo-Pacific are often at odds, placing ASEAN in a delicate position. China's Belt and Road Initiative (BRI) has significantly expanded its influence in the region through investments in infrastructure.

At the same time, the United States has renewed its focus on the Indo-Pacific, engaging through mechanisms like the Quad, including Australia, India, and Japan. ASEAN must carefully steer these relationships to maintain its neutrality and unity without aligning too closely with any single external power, ensuring its ability to mediate tensions and sustain regional stability.

The challenges faced by the APSC highlight the complexities of promoting political-security cooperation in a diverse and rapidly changing Southeast Asia. While ASEAN has made considerable strides in establishing frameworks for peace and stability, the evolving geopolitical environment, non-traditional security threats, and internal differences continue to test the region's cohesion and effectiveness. These challenges require adaptive strategies, deeper coordination, and an enhanced commitment to ASEAN's foundational principles of peace, security, and respect for sovereignty.

In short, the APSC is a cornerstone of ASEAN's vision to promote peace, stability, and security across Southeast Asia. By focusing on conflict resolution, political cooperation, and addressing traditional and non-traditional security challenges, the APSC has significantly fostered trust and collaboration among ASEAN member states and external partners. It has provided the framework for regional dialogue, promoting shared norms and responses to complex security dynamics in an evolving geopolitical landscape.

As ASEAN moves forward, the APSC must continue to adapt and strengthen its capacity to tackle emerging and multifaceted security challenges. This includes enhancing regional responses to cybersecurity threats, counterterrorism, transnational crime, and public health crises while managing longstanding concerns like territorial disputes and maritime security. The APSC's effectiveness in maintaining ASEAN's centrality in regional security discussions, promoting unity among its diverse members, and engaging external partners will be critical to the region's ability to manage these challenges. A proactive, resilient, and cohesive APSC will ensure Southeast Asia's long-term peace, stability, and security in an increasingly interconnected world.

> *"By fostering political security cooperation through mechanisms like the ASEAN Regional Forum and the East Asia Summit, ASEAN has ensured that political and security issues are addressed diplomatically. It is through these efforts that Southeast Asia remains one of the most politically stable regions in the world."*
>
> **Pushpanathan Sundram, Author**

Chapter 6

Social & Cultural Cooperation – The ASEAN Socio-Cultural Community

"The primary goal of the ASCC is to contribute to realising an ASEAN Community that is people-centred and socially responsible with a view to achieving enduring solidarity and unity among the nations and peoples of ASEAN by forging a common identity and building a caring and sharing society which is inclusive and harmonious where the well-being, livelihood, and welfare of the peoples are enhanced."

ASEAN Socio-Cultural Community Blueprint, June 2009, ASEAN Secretariat

While ASEAN is often recognised for its political and economic initiatives, the ASCC is a vital pillar that aims to create a people-centred and socially cohesive region. The ASCC embodies ASEAN's commitment to addressing the region's pressing social, cultural, and environmental challenges, with the overarching goal of enhancing the quality of life for all peoples of ASEAN.

Formally established as part of the ASEAN Charter in 2007, the ASEAN Socio-Cultural Community (ASCC) strives to cultivate a caring, inclusive, and harmonious community. This includes collaboration among member states to tackle common issues such as poverty alleviation, education enhancement, health improvement, environmental sustainability, and cultural preservation. As we explore this chapter, you will discover the key features and developmental journey of the ASCC, highlighting that ASEAN is making strides toward social justice, environmental protection, and cultural exchange. It's essential to recognise that these efforts are not just policies on paper; they have real implications for the lives of Southeast Asian people, ensuring that everyone benefits from regional integration.

Formation of ASCC

The mission for a socially inclusive and culturally vibrant ASEAN was first laid out in the ASEAN Vision 2020, where member states committed to advancing a region that balanced robust economic growth with social development and cultural preservation. This ambition became more explicit with the ASCC's formation in 2007 under the ASEAN Charter. The ASCC seeks to address the social, cultural, and environmental aspects of regional integration, focusing on the creation of a people-centred, socially responsible, and sustainable community. This vision is visible in the ASCC Blueprint 2025, which presents a thorough plan for accomplishing these goals, focusing on six key themes.

First, human development is important to the ASCC's aims, which include providing all people with access to quality education, lifelong learning opportunities, and workforce training. This strategy aspires to create a competent, competitive workforce capable of driving innovation and economic growth while encouraging social mobility and inclusivity. In recent years, ASEAN member states have made great strides in boosting school enrolment, enhancing access to technical and vocational education, and resolving educational inequities among regions.

The second is social welfare and protection, aiming to reduce poverty and inequality across member states. The ASCC emphasises the need to implement social safety nets, health care systems, and policies that support vulnerable groups, including those affected by poverty, unemployment, and health disparities. ASEAN's initiatives to improve social welfare are reflected in its growing focus on expanding healthcare access, promoting social protection programs, and enhancing support for marginalised communities. This is crucial for achieving balanced development across the region, as income and living standards disparities remain significant between and within ASEAN countries.

Promoting social justice and rights is the third focus area, which aims to protect the rights of vulnerable populations, including women, children, migrant workers, and persons with disabilities. The ASCC has advanced policies to support gender equality, child welfare, and the protection of migrant workers' rights, recognising that social justice is essential for fostering an inclusive and cohesive community. For example, the ASEAN Convention Against Trafficking in Persons (ACTIP) and the ASEAN Consensus on the Protection and Promotion of the Rights of Migrant Workers represent key frameworks to protect individuals from exploitation and support fair treatment.

Environmental sustainability forms the fourth cornerstone of the ASCC Blueprint. The region's rapid urbanisation and industrial growth have heightened environmental challenges such as climate change, deforestation, pollution, and natural resource depletion. ASEAN is committed to sustainable environmental practices by addressing these issues through regional cooperation and national policies. Initiatives to enhance environmental resilience include efforts to combat climate change, promote sustainable management of natural resources, and ensure food, water, and energy security. Notably, ASEAN has adopted the ASEAN Strategic Plan of Action on the Environment to encourage member states to adopt green technologies, reduce carbon emissions, and conserve biodiversity.

Building resilience is another priority, particularly in enhancing ASEAN's disaster preparedness and response capabilities. Southeast Asia is highly vulnerable to natural disasters, including typhoons, earthquakes, and floods, and this focus aims to reduce disaster risks and improve regional response mechanisms. ASEAN has strengthened its disaster management efforts through AADMER and the ASEAN Coordinating Centre for Humanitarian Assistance (AHA Centre), facilitating disaster response cooperation and promoting regional resilience.

Finally, cultural cooperation is essential to preserving ASEAN's diverse cultural heritage and fostering a sense of shared identity among member states. Efforts under this priority include promoting intercultural dialogue, protecting cultural heritage, and enhancing the role of culture in sustainable development. ASEAN has initiated programs to celebrate its diverse traditions, languages, and cultural expressions, such as the ASEAN Cultural Heritage Digital Archive and the annual ASEAN Cultural Festival. These programs aim to build a deeper sense of unity while respecting the distinct cultural practices of each member state.

Human development and education

Human development and education are central to the ASCC, which aims to improve access to education and promote lifelong learning across the region. Recognising education as the bedrock of human development, economic growth, and social cohesion, ASEAN has introduced a range of initiatives to enhance the quality and reach of educational opportunities for its citizens.

One of the ASCC's flagship programs is the ASEAN University Network (AUN). This initiative promotes academic collaboration, student mobility, and research partnerships among universities across the region. The AUN fosters a shared ASEAN identity and helps develop a regional pool of talent equipped to meet the demands of an increasingly interconnected and globalised world. By facilitating the exchange of ideas, students, and faculty, the AUN is a platform for cross-cultural understanding and collaborative innovation, strengthening regional integration through education.

However, this collaboration is not just superficial; ASEAN's commitment to lifelong learning and workforce development is particularly pertinent in the face of rapid technological change, which continues to reshape the global economy. The ASEAN Work Plan on Education (2021–2025) emphasises equipping the workforce with relevant skills for a knowledge-based economy, emphasising digital literacy, creativity, and critical thinking. A central focus of this work plan is the promotion of technical and vocational education and training (TVET), aimed at bridging skills gaps, improving employability, and fostering innovation. ASEAN's emphasis on TVET also addresses the needs of industries requiring specialised skills, aligning educational outcomes with labour market demands and economic development priorities.

Despite these efforts, disparities in access to quality education persist, particularly among the less developed ASEAN member states such as CLMV. These disparities manifest in infrastructure, teacher training, and educational outcomes. To address these challenges, ASEAN has prioritised capacity-building initiatives, including teacher training and curriculum development, and has sought financial assistance to improve educational infrastructure in these countries. Such measures are crucial for achieving equitable access to education and reducing regional disparities in human capital development.

The broader goal of the ASCC is to reduce social inequality and ensure inclusive development across ASEAN. Despite significant progress in poverty reduction over the past decades, social inequality remains a challenge. The ASCC's strategies promote inclusive economic growth, reduce disparities in access to basic services, and ensure that vulnerable populations are not left behind. The ASEAN Framework Action Plan on Rural Development and Poverty Eradication (2021–2025) serves as a roadmap for reducing poverty levels through rural development, enhancing access to social services such as healthcare and education, and supporting livelihood opportunities for marginalised communities.

It cannot be ignored that rural areas and marginalised groups, including indigenous peoples and migrant workers, continue to experience poverty and limited access to opportunities. The ASCC addresses these challenges by promoting social safety nets and developing comprehensive social protection systems that reduce vulnerability. ASEAN member states have introduced measures such as cash transfers, health insurance schemes, and employment support to enhance social welfare and ensure that all citizens have access to the resources they need to improve their quality of life.

It is worth noting that migrant workers significantly contribute to ASEAN's economic growth, yet they often face precarious conditions and vulnerabilities. Recognising their vital role, the ASCC has prioritised safeguarding their rights and welfare. The ASEAN Declaration on the Protection and Promotion of the Rights of Migrant Workers, adopted in 2007, established principles for fair treatment, access to social protection, and safe working conditions for migrant labour.

Building on this foundation, the ASEAN Consensus on the Protection and Promotion of the Rights of Migrant Workers provides a framework for member states to implement policies ensuring migrant workers' rights, protecting them from exploitation, and addressing issues related to human trafficking. These efforts are critical in fostering a fair and secure environment for migrant workers, who drive the region's economies and support regional integration.

ASEAN's efforts in human development, education, poverty reduction, and social protection reflect a holistic approach to fostering a more inclusive and cohesive regional community. By enhancing access to education, promoting social equity, and protecting the rights of vulnerable groups, the ASCC contributes to the vision of a people-centred and socially responsible ASEAN that balances economic progress with social well-being.

Social justice and human rights

The ASCC aims to tackle social inequality and promote inclusive development across the region. While notable strides have been made in poverty reduction over the years, social inequality continues to pose significant challenges. To address these issues, the ASCC implements strategies that foster inclusive economic growth, bridge disparities in access to essential services, and ensure that vulnerable populations are not overlooked. The ASEAN Framework Action Plan on Rural Development and Poverty Eradication (2021–2025) serves as a guiding roadmap for diminishing poverty levels through targeted rural development initiatives, improved access to healthcare and education, and support for livelihood opportunities in marginalised communities.

Despite progress, rural areas and marginalised groups—including Indigenous peoples and migrant workers—still struggle with poverty and limited opportunities. The ASCC proactively addresses these challenges by advocating for social safety nets and developing comprehensive social protection systems to reduce vulnerability. Various ASEAN member states have introduced initiatives such as cash transfers, health insurance schemes, and employment support, enhancing social welfare and ensuring that all citizens have access to the resources necessary to improve their quality of life.

Moreover, the ASCC emphasises the importance of gender equality and social justice. It seeks to combat issues such as gender-based violence, discrimination, and barriers to education and healthcare access. Through frameworks like the ASEAN Committee on Women (ACW) and the ASEAN Gender Mainstreaming Strategic Framework, ASEAN is committed to empowering women and girls, reducing educational and employment disparities, and promoting women's participation in regional decision-making processes.

The ASEAN Intergovernmental Commission on Human Rights (AICHR) is a critical component of ASEAN's commitment to human rights. As the primary mechanism for promoting and protecting human rights, AICHR serves as an advisory body, offering recommendations on human rights issues and raising awareness of human rights principles within ASEAN. Its focus encompasses the protection of vulnerable groups, the promotion of gender equality, and the prevention of violence and exploitation. However, AICHR's effectiveness is often limited by the principle of non-interference, which restricts its ability to intervene in domestic human rights matters.

Environmental sustainability and climate resilience

Environmental sustainability and climate resilience are critical priorities for ASEAN, given Southeast Asia's status as one of the most climate-vulnerable regions in the world. The region faces a wide array of environmental challenges, including deforestation, pollution, and the impacts of climate change, such as rising sea levels and increased frequency of extreme weather events. The ASCC plays a vital role in addressing these issues, fostering regional cooperation for environmental protection, promoting sustainable development, and enhancing climate resilience.

A significant environmental concern for ASEAN is transboundary haze pollution, which is primarily caused by the practice of slash-and-burn agriculture. This method, widely used for clearing land for palm oil plantations and other agricultural purposes, has led to severe air quality issues and has been a recurring problem for years, particularly affecting Indonesia, Malaysia, and Singapore. In response to the ongoing crisis, ASEAN adopted the ASEAN Agreement on Transboundary Haze Pollution (AATHP) in 2002—the first regional environmental treaty of its kind—to target the root causes of haze pollution, encourage sustainable land management practices and promote better coordination for fire prevention and suppression.

Despite the agreement and efforts made by countries, haze pollution persists as a major environmental and public health issue in the region. Episodes of transboundary haze lead to respiratory health problems, economic losses, and disruptions to daily life. The ASCC continues prioritising efforts to strengthen enforcement mechanisms under the agreement and bolster regional cooperation in mitigating haze effects. This includes promoting sustainable agricultural practices, enhancing early warning systems, and fostering greater collaboration among member states for fire monitoring and disaster response.

ASEAN's approach to environmental sustainability extends to broader climate resilience and disaster preparedness. Given the region's susceptibility to natural disasters like typhoons, floods, and droughts, enhancing climate resilience is central to the ASCC's agenda. The ASEAN Climate Change Initiative (ACCI) provides a framework for regional collaboration on climate change mitigation and adaptation. Under the ACCI, ASEAN member states work together to reduce greenhouse gas emissions, promote renewable energy, improve energy efficiency, and implement sustainable land use and forest management policies. These efforts are designed not only to reduce ASEAN's carbon footprint but also to build capacity for adapting to the adverse effects of climate change.

In parallel, the AHA Centre plays a key role in disaster response and humanitarian assistance. It coordinates regional disaster response efforts, facilitates the provision of emergency relief, and supports disaster preparedness and capacity building among ASEAN member states. Such coordination is crucial in a region that frequently experiences natural disasters, ensuring that resources are mobilised swiftly and effectively to respond to emergencies, minimise casualties, and support affected communities.

The ASCC Blueprint strongly emphasises disaster risk reduction, climate adaptation, and building resilience, particularly in communities most vulnerable to climate impacts, such as coastal areas and small island states. It recognises the need to strengthen resilience through integrated policies addressing disaster risk and long-term climate change impacts. The Blueprint encourages developing climate-resilient infrastructure, enhancing community-based adaptation practices, and integrating climate change considerations into national and local development planning.

ASEAN has also adopted principles of green growth and sustainable consumption and production (SCP) to advance environmental sustainability. These strategies aim to decouple economic growth from environmental degradation by promoting efficient resource use, reducing waste, and encouraging sustainable business practices. ASEAN has engaged in capacity-building initiatives, awareness campaigns, and policy frameworks to promote SCP across critical sectors, including energy, agriculture, and manufacturing.

Furthermore, ASEAN's environmental sustainability efforts align with global commitments to address climate change, such as the Paris Agreement, to which all member states are signatories. ASEAN countries have committed to reducing greenhouse gas emissions through nationally determined contributions (NDCs). They are working to enhance their climate commitments in line with global goals to limit temperature rise and foster sustainable development.

Cultural cooperation and carving ASEAN identity

Cultural cooperation is a central objective of the ASCC, aiming to cultivate a shared identity while celebrating the rich diversity of the region's cultures. The ASCC's efforts focus on promoting mutual understanding and solidarity across ASEAN's member states, which vary significantly in their traditions, languages, and customs. The ASCC creates a cohesive regional identity that respects and transcends national boundaries by encouraging cultural exchange and heritage preservation.

One of the primary areas of cultural collaboration facilitated by the ASCC is through its initiatives in culture and arts. The ASEAN Committee on Culture and Information (ASEAN-COCI) is at the forefront of these efforts, promoting cultural exchange and cooperation through various programs. These include arts festivals, cultural heritage preservation projects, and exchange programs encouraging the sharing of traditional knowledge and supporting the contemporary arts. Such initiatives help showcase Southeast Asia's diverse cultural expressions, from traditional music, dance, and crafts to modern visual and performing arts, offering opportunities for greater cultural awareness and interaction among ASEAN's populations.

Preserving the region's cultural heritage is vital, given the diverse range of ethnic communities, languages, and traditions in Southeast Asia. ASEAN-COCI's work includes safeguarding intangible cultural heritage, such as traditional crafts, rituals, and oral histories, ensuring that these practices are passed down to future generations. The emphasis on cultural preservation reflects ASEAN's commitment to valuing its diverse past while promoting creativity and cultural innovation within its societies.

The ASCC plays a pivotal role in fostering a broader sense of regional identity among the peoples of ASEAN. Beyond cultural preservation, initiatives to build an ASEAN identity have focused on promoting regional symbols and shared values that help strengthen the connection between citizens and the regional organisation. For instance, the adoption of the ASEAN Anthem, the display of the ASEAN Flag alongside national flags, and the annual celebration of ASEAN Day on August 8th are important reminders of the region's unity and shared aspirations. These symbols and commemorative events have become integral to building a collective identity, highlighting ASEAN's core objectives of unity, cooperation, and peace.

Educational programs and youth initiatives have been central to fostering a sense of belonging and regional identity, particularly among younger generations. Student exchange programs, youth forums, and leadership workshops have brought together young people from across ASEAN member states, offering opportunities to learn about different cultures, forge connections, and develop a deeper understanding of the commonalities and shared history within the region. These initiatives aim to build a new generation of ASEAN citizens who are aware of their regional identity and committed to ASEAN's solidarity and integration.

ASEAN's cultural and identity-building initiatives help preserve the region's diversity and contribute to social cohesion and regional integration. By emphasising shared values and fostering mutual respect, the ASCC aims to strengthen the bonds among Southeast Asian peoples and support the realisation of an integrated ASEAN community that embraces its cultural heritage while moving towards a shared future.

Challenges to ASCC

While the ASCC has made important strides in promoting social cohesion, cultural identity, and sustainable development, the barriers to realising its larger aims are substantial and diverse. The ASCC's aspirations are significant, but so are the challenges of solving social, economic, environmental, and human rights issues in such a diverse and quickly changing region.

Poverty and socioeconomic inequality remain a significant issue. Although poverty rates in Southeast Asia have decreased significantly in recent decades, there are still substantial differences in wealth distribution, social services, and opportunity. CLMV countries (Cambodia, Laos, Myanmar, and Vietnam) continue to have high poverty rates, undeveloped infrastructure, and limited access to excellent healthcare and education despite strong economic expansion in Singapore, Malaysia, and Thailand.

Urban-rural divides also exacerbate economic inequalities, with rural populations often lacking basic services such as clean water, sanitation, and educational facilities. The rise in income inequality, as measured by Gini coefficients in several ASEAN countries, further underscores the gap between the wealthy and marginalised communities.

Addressing these disparities requires economic growth, robust social protection mechanisms, and policies aimed at inclusive development. ASEAN's Framework Action Plan on Rural Development and Poverty Eradication is one such effort, focusing on rural livelihoods, gender equality, and community-based development; however, its success depends on member states' commitment to policy implementation and cross-border collaboration.

Environmental sustainability is another critical challenge for the ASCC, as Southeast Asia faces significant threats from deforestation, biodiversity loss, urban pollution, and climate change. The region is home to some of the most biodiverse habitats in the world, such as the Coral Triangle, yet it is also one of the fastest deforesting regions. Over the last few decades, significant tracts of forest have been lost to illegal logging, agricultural expansion (notably palm oil plantations), and infrastructure development. This deforestation threatens biodiversity and contributes to regional and global greenhouse gas emissions, impacting climate change.

Transboundary haze pollution, predominantly caused by forest fires and slash-and-burn agricultural practices in countries like Indonesia, has been a perennial problem affecting air quality, health, and economies across the region. While the AATHP of 2022 marked a regional commitment to address this issue, enforcement and compliance remain challenging, and the annual haze season continues to impact countries like Singapore, Malaysia, and Brunei.

Moreover, ASEAN's current energy mix heavily relies on coal and other fossil fuels, contributing to rising carbon emissions. Efforts such as the ASEAN Plan of Action for Energy Cooperation (APAEC) aim to promote renewable energy and improve energy efficiency; however, the transition to a low-carbon economy is still in its nascent stages and requires further investment in green technologies and sustainable practices. ASEAN's commitment to the Paris Agreement and the establishment of the ACCI provide frameworks for regional climate action. Yet, much remains to be done to build climate resilience, promote sustainable land-use practices, and shift toward a greener economy.

Furthermore, the region grapples with governance and policy coherence among its member states. The diversity of political systems—from democracies to other regimes—complicates efforts to forge a unified approach to social development and environmental protection. This diversity can lead to fragmented policy responses, as national interests and governance capacities vary significantly across ASEAN. For instance, while some member states prioritise economic liberalisation and rapid industrial development, others focus on social welfare or environmental sustainability.

The lack of binding enforcement mechanisms and reliance on consensus-based decision-making can lead to "lowest common denominator" agreements, where policies are diluted to achieve unanimous consent. While fostering unity and minimising conflict, this consensus approach often slows policy implementation and limits ASEAN's ability to respond decisively to pressing issues such as human trafficking, climate action, and labour rights.

Labour migration is another challenge that intersects with issues of social inequality, human rights, and regional economic integration. Millions of migrant workers move across ASEAN borders each year, contributing to the region's economic growth but also facing vulnerabilities such as labour exploitation, discrimination, and inadequate access to social protection. While ASEAN has adopted instruments like the ASEAN Consensus on the Protection and Promotion of the Rights of Migrant Workers, ensuring these standards are implemented across diverse legal and economic frameworks remains a significant challenge. The COVID-19 pandemic further exposed the precarity of migrant workers, as border closures, job losses, and lack of access to healthcare left many vulnerable to economic hardship and exploitation.

Lastly, building a shared ASEAN identity and social cohesion among its diverse member states remains a long-term aspiration for the ASCC. While cultural exchange programs, youth forums, and the promotion of ASEAN symbols have sought to foster a sense of regional belonging, national identities and linguistic, religious, and cultural differences continue to influence how communities perceive their relationship to the broader ASEAN community. The challenge lies in promoting regional identity without undermining national identities while leveraging ASEAN's diversity as a source of cultural richness and mutual understanding.

In essence, the ASCC is central to ASEAN's vision of a socially cohesive, culturally vibrant, and inclusive region that places people at the core of its development agenda. The ASCC has sought to improve access to education, reduce poverty, promote social welfare, address environmental challenges, and foster a shared regional identity. By enhancing human development, strengthening social protection mechanisms, and encouraging cultural cooperation, the ASCC aims to improve the quality of life for all ASEAN citizens and bridge socio-economic disparities across the region.

Despite progress in these areas, the ASCC faces several challenges, from poverty and social inequality to environmental sustainability, human rights, governance, labour migration, and regional identity. Addressing these issues requires a coordinated and sustained effort to strengthen regional frameworks, enhance policy coherence, and promote an inclusive, sustainable, and rights-based approach to social and cultural development in ASEAN. The ASCC's success will depend on its ability to navigate these intricacies while fostering a stronger, more resilient, and cohesive community for all of ASEAN's people.

Looking ahead, the ASCC must continue to address inequalities, ensure the protection of human rights while balancing state sovereignty, and enhance environmental sustainability. In doing so, the ASCC can help secure a people-centred ASEAN, ensuring that the benefits of regional integration are equitably shared and that the region's diverse populations thrive collectively.

> *"The ASEAN Socio-Cultural Community is the heart of ASEAN's vision for a people-centred and socially cohesive region. By fostering shared values, mutual understanding, and cooperation on social and cultural issues, the ASCC ensures that ASEAN's integration process benefits its people, strengthens resilience, and enhances the region's collective identity."*
>
> **Pushpanathan Sundram, Author**

Chapter 7

ASEAN's External Relations – Dialogue Partners & Regional Cooperation

> *"ASEAN itself became the hub for dialogue and communication....... All three countries — China, the Russian Federation, and the United States — have had the "comfort level" to allow ASEAN to take the lead in promoting a cooperative framework in the region."*
>
> **Marty Natalegawa,**
> **Does ASEAN Matter? A View From Within**

Since its inception, ASEAN has prioritised cultivating strong relationships with external partners, recognising that collaboration beyond its borders is essential for regional stability and prosperity. Over the years, ASEAN has established a rich network of partnerships with diverse dialogue partners, enabling it to enhance its role in regional affairs and effectively address shared challenges. ASEAN's approach to external relations is organised through several vital frameworks, including the ARF, PMCs, EAS, and APT. These mechanisms provide ASEAN a platform to engage with major global players like the

United States, China, and Russia. Through these partnerships, ASEAN tackles pressing regional issues such as territorial disputes, trade integration, and climate change, reinforcing its position as a vital player on the international stage.

This chapter will examine the dynamics of ASEAN's relationships with its dialogue partners and how these collaborations promote regional stability and economic cooperation. You will discover how ASEAN's evolving approach to managing its external relations ensures that it remains at the forefront of regional diplomacy, adapting to new challenges while fostering an inclusive environment for dialogue and partnership.

ASEAN Dialogue Partners

As of 2024, ASEAN maintains formal partnerships with 11 dialogue partners: Australia, Canada, China, the European Union, India, Japan, New Zealand, the Republic of Korea (South Korea), Russia, the United States, and the United Kingdom. Each partnership serves a different strategic purpose, reflecting ASEAN's multifaceted approach to diplomacy. In the following pages, I will briefly walk you through the nature and venues of these partnerships.

1974: Australia

As ASEAN's first Dialogue Partner since 1974, Australia has established deep economic, security, and cultural ties with the region. Economically, the AANZFTA remains a crucial framework, with two-way trade volume surpassing $101 billion in 2022. Australia is also an investor in ASEAN, with FDI flows reaching over $10 billion in the last decade.

Regarding strategic cooperation, it actively contributes to counterterrorism, maritime security, and defence collaboration through the ADMM-Plus and the ARF. Over 100,000 ASEAN students study in Australia annually, showcasing the strength of educational ties and people-to-people links. Australia provides substantial development assistance to ASEAN, focusing on disaster management, capacity-building, and climate change adaptation, aligning with regional needs and priorities.

1975: New Zealand

New Zealand has been a Dialogue Partner of ASEAN since 1975, focusing on sustainable development, agricultural cooperation, and fostering economic and security ties. Economically, the AANZFTA has facilitated robust economic engagement, with total ASEAN-New Zealand trade reaching about $14 billion in 2022.

On strategic cooperation, it actively supports ASEAN in peacekeeping, counterterrorism, and maritime security through forums such as the ARF. On a social and cultural level, it offers scholarships and various educational exchange programs to ASEAN students, contributing to people-to-people connectivity and knowledge sharing. It also provides development assistance across sectors like disaster management, climate resilience, and agricultural development.

1977: Japan

Japan, a Dialogue Partner since 1977, remains one of ASEAN's most important economic partners and its third-largest trading partner as of 2022. ASEAN-Japan trade volumes increased to over $268 billion in 2022, highlighting robust economic engagement facilitated by the AJCEP. Japan continues to be a significant investor in ASEAN, with FDI flows reaching around $27 billion in 2022, making it one of the region's top sources of foreign investment.

Strategic cooperation between ASEAN and Japan encompasses maritime security, disaster risk management, and infrastructure development. Japan also enhances people-to-people ties through programs like the Japan-East Asia Network of Exchange for Students and Youths (JENESYS). Furthermore, Japan's Official Development Assistance (ODA) to ASEAN exceeds $12 billion, focusing on infrastructure, technology transfer, and capacity building, emphasising fostering sustainable development and connectivity within the region.

1977: European Union

Since 1977, the European Union has been an ASEAN dialogue partner and continues to be one of its major economic partners. By 2022, it had become ASEAN's third-largest trading partner, with two-way trade volumes exceeding $295 billion, a substantial increase from previous years. The EU is also one of ASEAN's largest FDI sources, contributing approximately $24 billion in FDI in 2022.

The European Union-ASEAN strategic partnership includes critical areas such as cybersecurity, counterterrorism, and maritime security. In development cooperation, it actively supports sustainable development, human rights, and good governance through initiatives and funding programs. Initiatives like the European Union-ASEAN Young Leaders Forum and the Erasmus+ scholarships foster cultural and educational ties and promote greater people-to-people connectivity.

1977: United States

The United States, a Dialogue Partner since 1977, plays an important role in ASEAN's economic landscape. In 2022, it remained one of ASEAN's top FDI sources, contributing over $36 billion in FDI to the region. Economically, two-way trade grew to around $420 billion in 2022, reflecting the strong economic ties and trade partnership between the two regions. This substantial economic engagement underscores the United States' continued commitment to enhancing economic cooperation and partnership with ASEAN.

Strategically, it supports maritime security, counterterrorism, and disaster management through mechanisms like the ADMM-Plus. Social and cultural cooperation is extensive, with over 5,600 ASEAN students receiving Fulbright Scholarships. It also supports ASEAN through its foreign aid programs, focusing on governance, health, and economic development.

1977: Canada

Canada, which became an ASEAN dialogue Partner in 1977, focuses on development cooperation, inclusive governance, and advancing shared values. Between 2013-2022, bilateral trade flows reached approximately $20 billion, demonstrating growth and a commitment to economic partnership. Canada supports key areas in ASEAN, including education, gender equality, and climate resilience.

Canada and ASEAN have a strategic cooperation encompassing disaster risk reduction, environmental protection, and sustainable development. Canada's development assistance programs have contributed millions of dollars to ASEAN's rural development and peacebuilding initiatives and ongoing projects targeting areas like social protection, entrepreneurship, and climate change adaptation.

1989: South Korea

Since 1989, South Korea has been a key Dialogue Partner of ASEAN, contributing significantly to the region's economic and strategic development. Trade between the two regions was approximately $222 billion in 2022, supported by the AKFTA, which facilitates trade and investment between the two regions. South Korea remains a substantial investor in ASEAN's infrastructure, digital technology, and smart city initiatives, with FDI flows to ASEAN amounting to over $12 billion in 2022.

Strategically, it collaborates with ASEAN on regional security, maritime cooperation, and cybersecurity to address emerging security challenges. Socially, it enhances people-to-people connections by funding cultural exchange programs, scholarships, and initiatives like the ASEAN-Korea Centre, fostering deeper cultural and educational ties between the regions.

1996: China

Since becoming a Dialogue Partner in 1996, China has emerged as ASEAN's largest trading partner. By 2022, total bilateral trade exceeded $722 billion, reflecting the robust economic relationship driven by the ACFTA. It is also a key investor in ASEAN, contributing significantly to infrastructure development, technology, and manufacturing sectors. It collaborates strategically with ASEAN on maritime security, counterterrorism, and regional stability through the ARF and EAS mechanisms.

China's Belt and Road Initiative (BRI) has significantly impacted the region, financing infrastructure projects like roads, railways, and ports across ASEAN member states. Socially, people-to-people exchanges are strengthened through initiatives like the ASEAN-China Young Leaders

Scholarship and cultural exchange programs that enhance mutual understanding and connectivity.

1996: Russia

Russia has been an ASEAN Dialogue Partner since 1996, with key cooperation areas including energy security, defence cooperation, and strategic partnership. By 2022, bilateral trade reached approximately $15 billion, with growth seen particularly in sectors like energy, agriculture, and technology. While the trade volume remains modest compared to other partners, it continues to enhance its economic ties through investments in energy projects and arms trade with some ASEAN member states.

Strategically, it collaborates with ASEAN on counterterrorism, regional security, and non-traditional security through platforms like the ARF and the ASEAN Defence Ministers' Meeting-Plus (ADMM-Plus). It contributes to ASEAN's development through space technology, cybersecurity, and scientific cooperation initiatives while fostering cultural exchanges and educational partnerships supporting capacity-building and mutual understanding.

1996: India

India formalised its Dialogue Partner status with ASEAN in 1996, building on deep historical, cultural, and economic ties. Bilateral trade grew to approximately $113 billion in 2022, showcasing a growing partnership bolstered by AIFTA. India strongly emphasises enhancing digital connectivity, infrastructure development, and supply chain resilience in Southeast Asia. It engages in strategic cooperation covering maritime security, counterterrorism, and regional stability efforts through mechanisms like the ARF and the ADMM-Plus.

India's Act East Policy has been instrumental in strengthening economic ties, people-to-people connections, and cultural exchanges. It supports educational collaborations through programs like the ASEAN-India Research Training Fellowship and the ASEAN-India Scholarship for advanced research and capacity-building, deepening mutual understanding and cooperation across various sectors.

2021: United Kingdom

The United Kingdom (UK) became ASEAN's latest Dialogue Partner in 2021, marking a significant milestone in the region's external partnerships. As a new partner, it is actively increasing its engagement with ASEAN across multiple sectors, particularly in digital technology, green growth, and financial services. By 2022, two-way trade was valued at over $45 billion, demonstrating the growing regional economic ties. The UK is also expected to enhance its role in regional security cooperation, focusing on maritime security, cybersecurity, and counter-terrorism efforts through forums like the ARF.

The UK is a strong advocate for development cooperation in ASEAN. It focuses on climate action and supports the implementation of the SDGs. Initiatives include support for green finance, renewable energy, and sustainable infrastructure projects that align with ASEAN's goals for a greener, more sustainable future.

Preserving multipolarity through dialogue relations

Dialogue partnerships are critical to ASEAN's external relations, shaping its engagement with major global powers and fostering multifaceted cooperation. These partnerships are not just about economic ties; they encompass strategic security, political dialogue, historical connections, and socio-cultural exchanges. By establishing and nurturing dialogue partnerships, ASEAN ensures that its guiding principles, such as mutual respect and consensus-building, are maintained.

These relationships allow ASEAN to pursue a balanced approach in its external affairs, promote regional peace and stability, and provide platforms for collaboratively addressing global and regional challenges. Therefore, the process of selecting and upgrading dialogue partners is carefully considered, reflecting ASEAN's long-term vision for regional integration and international engagement.

Let me share an experience that illustrates the importance ASEAN places on these dialogue relationships. In 2010, as ASEAN deliberated on whether to invite the United States and Russia, both dialogue partners of ASEAN, to join the East Asia Summit (EAS), ASEAN officials tasked the ASEAN Secretariat with assessing the implications of this proposal. Both had indicated their interest in joining the forum. The EAS, established in 2005, had become a premier platform for dialogue on strategic, political, and economic matters in the Asia-Pacific region. By then, its membership included the ASEAN+6 countries: Australia, China, India, Japan, New Zealand, and South Korea. The prospect of expanding this exclusive forum to include two global powers required a careful evaluation of the benefits and potential challenges.

At the outset, we recognised that this was no ordinary decision. Including the United States and Russia in the EAS would signal a shift in the regional order, elevating the summit's global profile. Our assessment needed to address this proposal's strategic and operational dimensions as it may pose risks of diluting ASEAN's centrality in the forum.

We began by analysing the broader geopolitical context. The United States, under the Obama administration, had signalled a renewed focus on the Asia-Pacific through its "pivot to Asia" strategy. It sought deeper engagement with the region's institutions, and joining the EAS was an aspect of this approach. Russia, meanwhile, was reasserting its presence in global affairs and seeking stronger ties in Asia. For ASEAN, including these two powers, represented an opportunity to strengthen the EAS's role as an inclusive platform for major global players to discuss and address regional challenges. However, this had to be weighed against concerns about disrupting the delicate balance of power within the forum.

We assessed the strategic and operational implications of including the United States and Russia in the EAS. Strategically, their participation would strengthen the EAS's multipolar framework, aligning with ASEAN's vision of balanced power dynamics and providing opportunities to facilitate interactions among global powers. However, there were considerations, including potential dominance by these entrants, that could sideline ASEAN's priorities and impact ASEAN's centrality. Following rigorous scrutiny of the arguments, a consensus emerged in ASEAN that inviting the two powers was essential for ensuring the region's long-term stability and prosperity.

In late 2010, during the 5th East Asia Summit (EAS) in Hanoi, ASEAN leaders formally invited the United States and Russia to join the summit as full participants. This decision, culminating in their official participation at the 6th EAS in Bali in 2011, represented a pivotal moment in the forum's evolution. The inclusion of these two global powers not only expanded the EAS's strategic scope but also reflected ASEAN's adeptness at managing complex geopolitical dynamics.

The acceptance of the United States and Russia expanded the EAS into a platform for engaging all major powers in the Indo-Pacific. This move was strategically important, as it ensured the summit's relevance in addressing key regional and global issues, such as maritime security, economic integration, and climate change. It also reflected ASEAN's ability to foster an inclusive framework that balanced the interests of diverse stakeholders.

ASEAN successfully managed this expansion by reaffirming its centrality in shaping the region's strategic agenda. The EAS emerged as a critical forum for dialogue and cooperation, with ASEAN at its core. However, the decision also brought challenges, as the inclusion of these major powers heightened the complexity of maintaining unity within ASEAN amidst external pressures.

ASEAN Sectoral Dialogue Partners

ASEAN has established partnerships with several sectoral dialogue partners to foster cooperation in sectors such as economic development, environmental sustainability, and social-cultural exchanges. These partnerships complement ASEAN's broader external engagement strategy and reflect its approach of focusing on specific areas of cooperation. Thus, member states can leverage each partner's strengths to promote sustainable development, security, and social-cultural exchange.

1993: Pakistan

Pakistan became ASEAN's first sectoral dialogue partner in 1993, and the partnership has since focused on trade, investment, and economic cooperation. ASEAN-Pakistan bilateral trade has reached around $11 billion by 2022, showing steady growth. Its collaboration with ASEAN emphasises capacity-building, particularly in technology transfer, education, and sustainable development.

It collaborates with ASEAN on initiatives related to counterterrorism, anti-narcotics operations, and peacebuilding efforts in the region. Social and cultural exchanges are prominent in ASEAN-Pakistan relations. It offers higher education scholarships, cultural exchange programs, and training workshops to ASEAN students and professionals, focusing on closer people-to-people ties.

1999: South Africa

South Africa was made a sectoral dialogue Partner in 1999, further strengthening ties between Southeast Asia and Africa. The two-way trade between ASEAN and South Africa in 2022 was $8 billion. The trade focuses on sectors like manufacturing, mining and agriculture. The partnership promotes trade, investment, and economic cooperation, emphasising sustainable development, climate action, and knowledge-sharing on governance and public health. South Africa is crucial in enhancing South-South cooperation, aligning with ASEAN's goals for inclusive growth and regional stability. The partnership also includes joint efforts to address global challenges like climate change and sustainable infrastructure development.

2015: Norway

Norway became a sectoral dialogue partner in 2015, strongly emphasising sustainable development, ocean conservation, and climate change mitigation. It actively supports ASEAN's efforts in renewable energy and green technology investments, contributing to the region's move towards sustainability and low-carbon development. Economically, its investments in ASEAN's maritime industries, fisheries, and environmental protection initiatives have fostered stronger economic ties and collaboration in sustainable practices. It is also a key partner in advancing the region's human rights, good governance, and capacity-building programs, working closely with ASEAN to promote inclusivity, democratic governance, and responsible environmental stewardship.

2016: Switzerland

Switzerland formalised its sectoral dialogue partnership with ASEAN in 2016, focusing on economic cooperation, development assistance, and sustainable development. The relationship prioritises support for vocational education, small and medium-sized enterprises (SMEs), and financial inclusion within ASEAN member states, aiming to foster economic resilience and inclusive growth. It contributes to peace-building, human rights, and rule-of-law initiatives, offering technical expertise and capacity-building support. Social and cultural exchanges are a key aspect of the partnership. Switzerland promotes gender equality, inclusive development, and community-based projects that enhance people-to-people ties and further solidify ASEAN-Swiss relations.

2017: Turkey

Turkey became a sectoral dialogue partner in 2017, primarily focusing on trade, economic cooperation, and investment. Bilateral trade reached approximately $7.6 billion in 2022, driven by the infrastructure, construction, and manufacturing sectors. Turkey has actively invested in infrastructure development across ASEAN, contributing to regional connectivity and growth. It cooperates with ASEAN on counterterrorism, defence, and security cooperation issues, enhancing regional stability. Regarding development cooperation, it works closely with the AHA Centre to support disaster management and humanitarian efforts. Furthermore, it promotes cultural and educational exchanges to strengthen people-to-people connectivity, providing scholarships and opportunities for educational and cultural collaboration between Turkey and ASEAN member states.

2018: Brazil

Brazil formalised its sectoral dialogue partnership in 2018, focusing primarily on agriculture, food security, and trade relations. By 2022, the bilateral trade reached over $33 billion, mainly driven by Brazil's export of soybeans, poultry, and other agricultural products to ASEAN markets. It also engages with ASEAN in bioenergy projects, sustainable agriculture, and environmental protection, specifically emphasising biodiversity conservation and promoting sustainable practices in both regions. A world of sports diplomacy, cultural exchanges, and educational programs characterises the partnership with Brazil, enhancing people-to-people ties and mutual understanding between ASEAN member states and Brazil.

2021: Morocco

ASEAN established a sectoral dialogue partnership with Morocco in 2021, marking its first partnership in Africa. Morocco's collaboration with ASEAN focuses on strengthening socio-economic cooperation, particularly in trade, investment, and agriculture. Morocco also contributes to ASEAN's development goals by sharing expertise in renewable energy and sustainable agriculture. The partnership promotes knowledge exchange on governance, infrastructure, and climate resilience. Morocco's engagement in ASEAN further strengthens South-South cooperation, fostering closer ties between the African continent and Southeast Asia.

2022: United Arab Emirates

The United Arab Emirates (UAE) became a sectoral dialogue partner of ASEAN in 2022, focusing on enhancing economic, trade, and investment ties between the Gulf and Southeast Asia. Trade recorded a whopping $65 billion in 2022, with modern and much-needed collaboration on renewable energy, agriculture and the digital economy. Cooperation between ASEAN and the UAE spans energy, renewable resources, infrastructure development, and digital transformation. The partnership also supports education, technology, and innovation initiatives, contributing to ASEAN's sustainable development and regional integration efforts. The UAE's involvement underscores a growing economic and strategic link between the two regions.

ASEAN Development Partners

ASEAN's development partners contribute significantly to the region's socio-economic progress, environmental sustainability, and capacity-building efforts. These partnerships target sustainable development, climate change adaptation, infrastructure development, and public health. ASEAN's cooperation with its Development Partners is vital in addressing the region's complex development challenges. These partnerships contribute to economic growth and infrastructure development, long-term sustainability goals, climate resilience, and human rights advocacy. By leveraging the financial and technical expertise of its development partners, ASEAN ensures its member states can pursue economic and environmental stability in a rapidly changing world.

2009: Germany

Germany became an ASEAN development partner in 2009, strongly focusing on sustainable development, environmental conservation, and vocational education. Through programs like the ASEAN-German Cooperation on Climate Action and Biodiversity Conservation, Germany supports ASEAN's efforts in climate change mitigation, energy efficiency, and the development of renewable energy sources. This partnership also promotes sustainable urban development, enhances environmental protection, and advances clean energy.

In addition, Germany plays a pivotal role in establishing good governance, human rights, and peace-building efforts across the ASEAN region. The collaboration emphasises technical and vocational training (TVET) to strengthen the skills of ASEAN's young workforce, aiming to enhance employability and economic growth through programs like the RECOTVET (Regional Cooperation Programme on Technical and Vocational Education and Training).

2021: Chile

Chile established a development partnership in 2021, focusing on enhancing cooperation in sustainable development, trade, climate change, and education. The partnership promotes knowledge exchange and technical expertise, particularly in renewable energy and digital economy initiatives. Chile's involvement with ASEAN strengthens economic integration efforts and aligns with ASEAN's long-term goals in capacity-building and infrastructure development. By leveraging its expertise in green energy and digital innovation, Chile contributes to regional sustainability and socio-economic progress.

2022: France

France became a development partner in 2022, fostering cooperation in sustainable development, climate action, the digital economy, and education. This partnership emphasises joint efforts in addressing global challenges, including climate change mitigation, biodiversity conservation, and renewable energy. France's support also extends to infrastructure development and technical training, aligning with ASEAN's socio-economic and environmental goals. The partnership enhances ASEAN's capacity-building initiatives and strengthens its regional integration efforts.

2022: Italy

Italy formalised its development partnership with ASEAN in 2022, emphasising collaboration in sectors such as sustainable development, climate action, innovation, and education. The partnership focuses on green technology, infrastructure, and renewable energy initiatives, contributing to ASEAN's efforts to enhance regional resilience and socio-economic progress. Italy also supports ASEAN's digital transformation and capacity-building programs, providing expertise in areas like industrial development and environmental protection. This cooperation aligns with ASEAN's goals of long-term sustainability and regional integration.

2022: Netherlands

The Netherlands became a development partner in 2022, focusing on joint efforts in sustainable development, climate resilience, and water management. This partnership supports ASEAN's goals in renewable energy, environmental protection, and sustainable urban development. The Netherlands also contributes to capacity-building in areas like education, infrastructure, and public health, providing technical expertise and financial assistance. Collaboration between ASEAN and the Netherlands aligns with regional priorities, enhancing socio-economic growth and long-term sustainability.

2024: Peru

Peru established a development partnership with ASEAN in 2024, focusing on enhancing cooperation in trade, sustainable development, and capacity-building. This partnership supports ASEAN's efforts in environmental conservation, renewable energy, and economic integration, strongly emphasising climate change mitigation and biodiversity protection. Peru also contributes to knowledge-sharing in agriculture, public health, and disaster risk management. The ASEAN-Peru partnership strengthens ties between Southeast Asia and Latin America, promoting shared goals in sustainable development and regional cooperation.

External relations mechanisms

Beyond its relationships with individual dialogue partners, ASEAN has established several key mechanisms to manage its external relations effectively. These platforms enable ASEAN to engage in multilateral discussions regarding regional security, economic cooperation, and political stability, ensuring it remains a significant player in the evolving Asia-Pacific landscape. One of the vital mechanisms is the Post Ministerial Conferences (PMCs), which serve as essential platforms for ASEAN's bilateral and multilateral dialogue with its dialogue partners. Simply put, these are meetings between ASEAN as a bloc and each of its individual dialogue partners.

The PMC+1 format facilitates annual discussions between ASEAN Foreign Ministers and each dialogue partner, addressing mutual concerns across political, economic, and security domains while setting the direction for future cooperation. Conversely, the PMC+10 format allows ASEAN to engage collectively with all ten dialogue partners, providing a comprehensive platform for discussions on regional and global developments. These conferences reaffirm ASEAN's role in regional diplomacy and strengthen its external relations through inclusive and constructive engagement.

The ASEAN Plus Three (APT) framework, initiated in 1997 and comprising ASEAN, China, Japan, and South Korea, has produced several notable initiatives to foster economic integration and financial cooperation. Among its significant achievements is the CMIM, which serves as a regional financial safety net to provide liquidity during times of financial crisis. The ASEAN Plus Three Emergency Rice Reserve (APTERR) is critical in ensuring regional food security, especially during crises. The AMRO supports macroeconomic research and surveillance, bolstering regional economic stability. Furthermore, the APT framework has prioritised pandemic preparedness, advancing public health cooperation, and building resilience against future crises, all while promoting trade liberalisation and infrastructure connectivity.

The East Asia Summit (EAS), established in 2005, stands as a premier platform for ASEAN's external engagement with key partners. The EAS comprises ASEAN's ten member states and eight dialogue partners: the United States, China, Japan, India, Russia, Australia, New Zealand, and South Korea. This forum serves as a strategic dialogue platform addressing various regional and international issues impacting the Asia-Pacific region, covering regional security, maritime cooperation, economic integration, and transnational challenges like climate change, natural disasters, and pandemics.

ASEAN plays a proactive role in setting the EAS agenda and driving dialogue, reinforcing its centrality in regional diplomacy. The annual EAS Leaders' Summit is a key event where heads of state and government engage in open discussions on these strategic issues, promoting peace, stability, and prosperity in the region. Through these mechanisms, ASEAN strengthens its external relations and solidifies its position as a critical actor in shaping the regional and global governance landscape.

Ensuring ASEAN's centrality in the East Asia Summit

From its inception, ensuring ASEAN's centrality in the EAS was a key priority, reflecting the bloc's vision for regional leadership. While the EAS is a Leader-Led forum, ASEAN's role as the coordinator and driving force had to be firmly established to avoid any erosion of its influence. My experience as Director of External Relations at the ASEAN Secretariat during the first EAS in 2005 offers insight into the delicate negotiations and strategic decisions that shaped this centrality.

Preparations for the inaugural EAS were intense, with numerous meetings and documents to draft. Among these, the Chairman's Statement of the 1st EAS Summit held particular importance. It was not just a ceremonial document but a precedent-setting declaration meant to define the tone and framework for how the EAS would operate. As the individual tasked with drafting this statement, I understood its significance in embedding ASEAN's leadership into the DNA of the EAS process.

The EAS was designed to include ASEAN and its six dialogue partners at the time—China, Japan, South Korea, India, Australia, and New Zealand. However, a challenge emerged early in the drafting process: representatives from non-ASEAN member states suggested listing all EAS participants alphabetically in the Chairman's Statement. At first glance, this seemed a reasonable and neutral proposal, reflecting equality among members. However, it raised a deeper concern: such a move could symbolically diminish ASEAN's central role as the convener and coordinator of the EAS.

Alphabetical listing might have seemed trivial, but symbolism matters in diplomacy. ASEAN needed to be explicitly recognised as the summit's driving force—not merely one participant among equals. This required a strategic approach. While ASEAN's name conveniently begins with "A," I took steps to ensure this order reflected more than coincidence. I emphasised ASEAN's unique role in initiating and steering the summit through informal consultations and bilateral discussions with EAS representatives. The goal was to secure explicit acknowledgement of ASEAN's leadership both in the document's wording and structure.

Eventually, consensus was achieved. ASEAN was placed first in the list of EAS members, not merely due to alphabetical order but as a deliberate affirmation of its centrality. This decision may appear minor, but it carries significant symbolic weight. It established a precedent for future EAS statements and ensured that ASEAN's leadership role was enshrined in both form and substance.

The strategic placement of ASEAN in the inaugural Chairman's Statement was part of a broader effort to maintain its influence amidst an increasingly complex regional landscape. As the EAS evolved, welcoming major powers such as the United States and Russia in 2011, ASEAN's centrality continued to be tested. However, the foundational work done during the first summit played a critical role in reinforcing ASEAN's position as the primary architect and coordinator of the EAS framework.

This experience highlights how even seemingly minor decisions can have far-reaching implications in international diplomacy. By ensuring ASEAN's leadership was explicitly recognised, we safeguarded its ability to steer the summit's dynamics and retain its pivotal role in shaping the region's strategic architecture.

ASEAN Regional Forum

Established in 1994, the ASEAN Regional Forum (ARF) is one of Asia-Pacific's most important multilateral security forums. It comprises ASEAN member states, dialogue partners, and other key regional actors and provides a platform for discussing various security issues, including maritime security, counterterrorism, cyber security, and conflict resolution.

The ARF plays a crucial role in confidence-building measures and preventive diplomacy. It promotes open dialogue on contentious issues such as the South China

Sea disputes, nuclear non-proliferation, and disaster relief operations. By fostering cooperation and mutual trust among its participants, it aims to enhance regional peace and stability.

The ARF's annual ministerial meetings and working groups address emerging security challenges, aligning with ASEAN's goal of maintaining a rules-based regional order. The 31st ARF held in July 2024 emphasised multilateral cooperation on emerging security challenges, reinforcing ASEAN's goal of maintaining peace, stability, and a rules-based order in the region.

ASEAN's evolving role in global governance

One of ASEAN's most significant achievements is maintaining peace and stability in Southeast Asia. By establishing platforms like the ARF, PMCs, APT and EAS, ASEAN has positioned itself as an advocate for dialogue on critical regional security issues. These mechanisms have been instrumental in preventing conflict escalation, building trust, and fostering cooperation among major regional powers.

Economically, ASEAN has made remarkable progress in advancing regional trade and investment by forming the AEC and its numerous FTAs with dialogue partners. These initiatives have facilitated greater economic integration within ASEAN and with external partners, boosting the region's growth and competitiveness on the global stage. As ASEAN strengthens its economic links, its ability to engage effectively with global partners will be crucial to sustaining its economic dynamism.

However, as ASEAN expands its network of external partners, it faces the challenge of maintaining its centrality amid an increasingly complex geopolitical landscape. The rise of China, the evolving policies of the United States, and the growing influence of regional powers such as India and Japan are reshaping the dynamics of the Asia-Pacific. For ASEAN to continue serving as the primary regional dialogue and cooperation platform, it must skilfully manage these shifting power balances while preserving its unity and cohesion. ASEAN's ability to remain involved in regional security, economic cooperation, and regional governance discussions will be essential to its long-term relevance and success in global governance.

ASEAN's external relations reflect its ability to strike a delicate balance between regional priorities and global engagement. ASEAN has become a vital player in Asia-Pacific by forging strategic partnerships with dialogue partners and asserting its centrality in key forums like the ARF and EAS. As the global environment shifts, ASEAN's ability to stay agile, tackle emerging challenges, and uphold its founding principles of peace, stability, and economic cooperation will define its future. More than ever, ASEAN's resilience, adaptability, and commitment to multilateralism will secure its future position as a critical force driving regional prosperity and global dialogue.

Looking ahead, ASEAN's strength lies in its capacity to bring together diverse nations and foster collaboration on critical issues like climate change, regional security, and digital transformation. This cohesive approach ensures that ASEAN responds to immediate challenges and paves the way for sustainable and long-term regional growth. In an era of growing global uncertainties, ASEAN's ability to lead diplomatically, harness partnerships, and advocate for its collective interests will be crucial to its enduring relevance and influence on the global stage.

By keeping its core values at the heart of its initiatives and evolving to meet the demands of a changing world, ASEAN ensures that it becomes not just a regional player but a significant interlocuter in shaping the future of international relations.

> *"External relations have positioned ASEAN as a central player in the evolving regional architecture through its dialogue partnerships and regional cooperation mechanisms. By engaging major powers and fostering multilateral cooperation, ASEAN ensures that Southeast Asia remains stable, open, and integrated into the global economy. These partnerships enhance ASEAN's strategic leverage while maintaining its core principle of neutrality."*
>
> **Pushpanathan Sundram, Author**

Chapter 8

ASEAN's Economic Future: Integration, Trade, & Innovation

"Taking lessons from the severe disruptions from the pandemic and global developments, ASEAN will need to give greater focus to ensure regional resilience for a more sustainable and future-proof community. There is no better time than now for us to start looking at a new approach to economic integration.... We have many reasons to be optimistic. ASEAN has been able to successfully navigate the turbulent world by taking collective actions in establishing a resilient economic community."

ASEAN Secretary-General Lim Jock Hoi, ASEAN Economic Integration Brief, December 2022, ASEAN Secretariat

In recent years, disruptive events like the COVID-19 pandemic have changed the global economic environment, exposing supply chain vulnerabilities and emphasising the crucial need for regional cooperation. The pandemic acted as a sobering lesson for ASEAN countries to work together on public health, accelerate economic recovery, and strengthen resilience to future shocks. This urgency mirrors a broader global trend in which regional collaboration is critical for addressing complicated challenges.

The epidemic highlighted the interdependence of ASEAN economies. As border closures and supply chain disruptions reverberated throughout the area, it became evident that increasing intra-regional commerce and protecting investment flows were not just strategic objectives but economic imperatives. In response, the Association created the ASEAN Comprehensive Recovery Framework (ACRF), a plan for collaborative action to rebuild economies and increase resilience. The ACRF offers important methods for creating a more robust and adaptive economic environment, including supporting digital transformation, promoting long-term recovery, and improving social protection measures.

As Asia traverses an increasingly multipolar world, ASEAN's strategic position and collective power play a key role in shaping global economic governance. The Association is uniquely positioned to serve as a link between emerging economies and established powers, enabling trade and investment flows and promoting regional economic integration. This proactive approach demonstrates the group's will to determine its economic destiny in the face of changing global dynamics.

Exploring ASEAN's most recent economic strategy necessitates a comprehensive grasp of the complex environment of intra-regional trade, the transformational impact of digital innovation, and the changing character of trade agreements. By carefully positioning itself inside global trade frameworks, ASEAN proves that the ASEAN Economic Community (AEC) is more than just an aspiration but a dynamic process that drives growth and innovation. This vision will change Southeast Asia's economic environment, cementing its position as a key player in the global economy. But it is not as simple as it may look; let's explore why!

Achievements and evolving challenges

Since its inception, the AEC has laid the groundwork for ASEAN's economic integration, enhancing the free flow of goods, services, capital, investment, and skilled labour. Over the years, it has led to significant progress in reducing trade barriers, liberalising the service sector, and enhancing regional connectivity. In 2022, intra-ASEAN trade reached $830 billion, accounting for around 22% of the region's total trade volume, with leading industries being electronics, machinery, and agricultural products.

The FDI landscape has also been promising despite the COVID-19 pandemic surge, with ASEAN attracting $212 billion in 2021. Key sectors driving this investment include manufacturing, digital services, and infrastructure development, underscoring the region's economic vibrancy. This influx of FDI highlights ASEAN's attractiveness as a hub for multinational corporations looking to tap into the region's growing markets and skilled workforce. The region's young population and increasing consumer spending position ASEAN as a dynamic business marketplace.

Trade and investment liberalisation

ASEAN's Trade in Goods Agreement (ATIGA), signed in 2009, has played a critical role in expanding intra-regional trade by eliminating about 99% of tariffs on traded goods. This transformative agreement has enabled the efficient movement of goods across the region, facilitated by streamlined customs procedures and the ASW. In 2022, the ASW reduced average customs clearance times by 30-40%, enhancing overall trade efficiency and generating business cost savings.

The ability to expedite trade processes is vital in a world increasingly focused on speed and efficiency. This allows businesses to respond swiftly to market demands. Furthermore, the ASW has facilitated better coordination among customs authorities, promoting transparency and predictability in cross-border trade. This becomes crucial as businesses operate in a competitive global environment where time to market can significantly impact profitability.

On the other hand, the ASEAN Trade in Services Agreement (ATISA) signed in 2020 is a pivotal framework designed to enhance service trade among ASEAN member states. The ATISA aims to create a more integrated services sector by addressing barriers to trade in various service industries, including financial services, telecommunications, and healthcare. This agreement recognises that services are critical to the region's economic development, contributing significantly to GDP and employment.

ATISA's key provisions focus on liberalising service sectors, ensuring that professionals can move freely across borders with minimal restrictions. For example, by promoting mutual recognition of qualifications, ATISA facilitates the mobility of skilled workers such as engineers, nurses, and architects, thereby addressing labour shortages in critical sectors. Such liberalisation is expected to enhance the competitiveness of ASEAN economies by allowing them to leverage each other's human capital and expertise.

Additionally, ATISA encompasses sectors crucial for the digital economy, including information technology and e-commerce. By streamlining regulations and reducing barriers, ATISA encourages investment in digital services, enabling ASEAN to tap into the growing global digital economy, which is projected to reach $16.5 trillion by 2028. Moreover, ATISA promotes regulatory cooperation among member states. By harmonising regulations and standards, ASEAN can create a more predictable environment for service providers, encouraging investment and innovation. This agreement is expected to enhance regional competitiveness, allowing ASEAN to position itself as a hub for service industries in Asia.

On the investment front, the ASEAN Comprehensive Investment Agreement (ACIA), signed in 2009, is a cornerstone of ASEAN's investment framework. It aims to create a more conducive environment for FDI by providing greater protection and transparency for investors. ACIA addresses various issues, including expropriation, dispute resolution, and transfer of funds, ensuring that investors can confidently operate across member states. Moreover, by promoting more significant investment in priority sectors such as infrastructure, renewable energy, and technology, ACIA aligns with ASEAN's broader sustainable economic development goals.

The ACIA has contributed to increasing FDI in ASEAN, which reached close to $226 billion in 2023, 17% of global FDIs continuing the region's strong performance post-pandemic from 2022, when FDI inflows hit USD 224 billion. This marks a modest increase of 1.2% year-on-year despite global economic uncertainties. ASEAN's almost one-fifth share of global FDI underscores its continued attractiveness as a top destination for investment. The United States remained the largest contributor to ASEAN's FDI inflows, accounting for 32% in 2023, driven by factors like supply chain shifts and "friend-shoring" strategies.

Challenges and future path

Despite its gains, ASEAN faces significant difficulties. Reducing NTBs, attaining regulatory harmonisation, and closing the development gap between more advanced economies like Singapore and Malaysia and less developed countries like Laos and Myanmar are all crucial. NTBs, such as different standards for food safety and consumer protection, impede commerce, notably in agricultural and manufactured goods. According to a 2022 ASEAN assessment, NTBs account for approximately 35% of regional trade expenses, making them a major problem for policymakers. The disparity in standards and regulations among member states results in a fragmented trade environment, restricting the potential for closer economic integration. For example, inconsistencies in food safety regulations can cause delays in the clearance of agricultural products, affecting supply chains and farmers' market access.

Removing NTBs is critical to a more competitive and integrated ASEAN economy. Member states can improve the efficiency of cross-border transactions by harmonising legislation and standards. The World Bank predicts that eliminating NTBs may boost intra-ASEAN trade by up to 20%, resulting in significant economic gains for all member nations. The ASEAN Trade Facilitation Framework is a specific initiative for removing NTBs. It promotes member states to use best practices in customs procedures, such as simplified clearance processes and transparent laws. This program has the potential to significantly improve trade efficiency and reduce costs for businesses in the region.

Addressing these challenges is paramount for ensuring that all member states can benefit from economic integration. The Master Plan on ASEAN Connectivity 2025

(MPAC 2025) is a significant initiative to address these disparities by enhancing physical and institutional connectivity across ASEAN. Considerable investments are needed to improve transport networks, energy grids, and digital infrastructure, fostering a more cohesive economic environment. For example, the Asian Development Bank (ADB) estimates that ASEAN will need to invest approximately $210 billion annually in infrastructure to sustain its growth trajectory. This investment will enhance connectivity and support sustainable development goals, addressing climate change and environmental sustainability issues. The focus on green infrastructure is particularly relevant to the region's increasing environmental challenges.

In addition to infrastructure challenges, regulatory harmonisation remains a critical focus. Differences in regulatory frameworks across member states can create barriers to trade and investment. A concerted effort is required to streamline regulations and standards, particularly in sectors vital for regional integration, such as food safety, pharmaceuticals, and consumer protection.

Enhancing regional and global markets

ASEAN has forged several important FTAs to enhance regional economic integration and broaden access to global markets. These agreements have significantly expanded ASEAN's economic footprint beyond the region, creating trade, investment, and innovation opportunities. The signing of the RCEP in 2020 was a landmark moment, making the world's largest trade agreement by economic size. RCEP encompasses 30% of global GDP and 28% of international trade, integrating ASEAN with five major dialogue partners: China, Japan, South Korea, Australia, and New Zealand. According to China's Ministry of Commerce, the RCEP's intra-regional trade turnover is said to have reached nearly $5.6 trillion in 2023, illustrating the potential benefits of deeper economic integration.

One of the critical aspects of RCEP is the harmonisation of rules of origin, which simplifies the process for businesses to qualify for preferential tariffs across the members. RCEP also covers intellectual property, e-commerce, and investment protection, setting standards for cooperation in various sectors. As of 2023, all 15 signatory countries have ratified the agreement, marking its full implementation. RCEP is projected to generate a net gain of $245b billion in global income annually by 2030, with ASEAN members poised to benefit significantly from enhanced access to regional supply chains.

In addition to RCEP, ASEAN has established several key FTAs with its dialogue partners, significantly enhancing its economic integration and regional trade dynamics. The ACFTA has been particularly influential, solidifying China's status as ASEAN's largest trading partner. This agreement has facilitated tariff reductions and enhanced cooperation in various sectors, promoting a robust exchange of goods and services.

Similarly, the AJCEP has been vital in fostering economic ties between ASEAN and Japan. The AJCEP focuses on crucial areas such as technology transfer, sustainable energy projects, and infrastructure development. This partnership bolsters trade and encourages investments that enhance regional connectivity and sustainable practices. Notably, Japan has been a significant source of investment in ASEAN, particularly in technology and infrastructure projects. The AKFTA is another cornerstone of ASEAN's trade strategy, emphasising collaboration in manufacturing and technology. The AKFTA encourages partnerships that leverage South Korea's technological advancements and manufacturing capabilities, further integrating these economies.

The AIFTA has enhanced cooperation across various sectors, including information technology, pharmaceuticals, and services. AIFTA opens avenues for collaboration that leverage India's growing economic influence and ASEAN's diverse market potential. Lastly, the AANZFTA fosters cooperation in agriculture, education, manufacturing, and services, encouraging investment flows and creating a more interconnected economic environment. Through these strategic FTAs, ASEAN fortifies its position within the global trade landscape and cultivates diverse economic partnerships that enhance resilience and adaptability in an ever-evolving economic climate. These agreements reflect ASEAN's commitment to fostering an integrated, competitive, and sustainable economic region. They have contributed significantly to ASEAN's economic growth and positioned the region as a central economic hub in the Asia-Pacific.

While ASEAN's trade agreements have garnered growth, modernisation is crucial to addressing emerging issues such as digitalisation, sustainability, and supply chain resilience. Efforts to update ATIGA are ongoing, aiming to incorporate digital trade facilitation, environmental standards, and mechanisms for addressing non-tariff measures (NTMs). This evolution will ensure that trade agreements remain responsive to the rapidly changing global economy.

Digital economy: a game changer for ASEAN

The digital economy is becoming a major growth driver within ASEAN and is projected to exceed $330 billion by 2025. The COVID-19 pandemic significantly accelerated this transformation, with surging growth in e-commerce, fintech, and online services. In 2022, the value of ASEAN's digital economy was estimated at $194 billion, with leading players like Indonesia, Vietnam, and Thailand leading the way in digital adoption.

The ASEAN Digital Integration Framework was adopted in 2018 to support this growth, establishing a roadmap to build a connected digital ecosystem. Key priorities include promoting cross-border e-commerce, improving the interoperability of digital payments, and enhancing cybersecurity cooperation. Establishing an ASEAN-wide e-commerce platform and payment system connectivity is critical for boosting online trade and reducing transaction costs. Despite the rapid expansion of the digital economy, disparities in digital infrastructure and access persist across member states. While Singapore and Malaysia lead in ICT infrastructure, countries like Cambodia, Laos, and Myanmar need more broadband connectivity and digital literacy. Addressing this digital divide through investments in infrastructure and capacity-building is essential for ensuring inclusive growth.

The digital economy presents vast opportunities for ASEAN, driven by increasing internet penetration and rising consumer demand. The fintech sector is also flourishing, with over 400 startups across ASEAN providing digital banking, payments, and blockchain solutions, particularly benefiting underbanked and rural populations. These innovations empower consumers and enhance financial inclusion, making it crucial for ASEAN to foster a supportive regulatory environment that encourages innovation and entrepreneurship.

Building supply chain resilience and regionalisation

The disruptions caused by the COVID-19 pandemic and rising geopolitical tensions have exposed vulnerabilities in global supply chains, prompting a shift towards regionalisation. ASEAN's strategic location, competitive labour costs, and improving infrastructure make it a prime destination for supply chain diversification. Countries like Vietnam, Thailand, and Indonesia are becoming key players in electronics manufacturing, automotive production, and textile exports. Vietnam, in particular, has benefitted from the "China Plus One" strategy, as multinational companies shift production to diversify risk. Enhancing connectivity through initiatives like the ASW and MPAC 2025 aims to improve logistics and customs efficiency and reduce transaction costs, making ASEAN more attractive for global businesses and investors.

The need for supply chain resilience has also led ASEAN countries to focus on localising production and sourcing. The rise of "nearshoring"—relocating production closer to end markets—presents opportunities for ASEAN to attract companies looking to mitigate risks associated with long-distance supply chains. For instance, the increasing demand for electronic components amidst global semiconductor shortages has prompted investments in local manufacturing capabilities across the region. Moreover, the ASEAN grouping is uniquely positioned to capitalise on shifts in global supply chains. As global companies seek alternatives to China for manufacturing and sourcing, ASEAN's diverse economies offer a compelling mix of capabilities, resources, and markets. This evolution enhances economic resilience and strengthens ASEAN's standing in the global economic landscape.

Engaging in global trade frameworks: navigating the future

ASEAN's engagement with global trade frameworks, such as the Comprehensive and Progressive Agreement for Trans-Pacific Partnership (CPTPP) and the Indo-Pacific Economic Framework (IPEF), will be crucial for its economic strategy. The CPTPP sets high standards for intellectual property, labour rights, and environmental protections, while ASEAN's participation in this framework will enhance access to global markets and promote sustainable trade practices.

Conversely, the IPEF, launched by the United States in 2022, offers a platform for deeper engagement in digital trade, clean energy, and supply chain resilience. ASEAN must balance its participation in IPEF against its existing economic ties with China and other key partners to maintain strategic autonomy. Navigating these complex trade agreements will be pivotal for ASEAN to maximise its benefits while mitigating potential risks associated with over-reliance on any single partner. ASEAN's role as a mediator and facilitator in trade is essential for maintaining stability in a rapidly changing geopolitical environment. By actively engaging in international trade frameworks, ASEAN can enhance its influence and advocate for the interests of its member states in the global arena.

The acceptance of partner status with BRICS (Brazil, Russia, India, China, South Africa) grouping by Indonesia,

Malaysia, Thailand, and Vietnam in October 2024 brings multifaceted implications for the AEC. On the positive side, joining BRICS could offer these ASEAN nations a chance to diversify their economic partnerships beyond traditional Western markets, paving the way for new trade agreements and collaborative ventures to stimulate growth in selected areas. The 23 BRICS economies, including members and partners, represent over $28.5 trillion or about 28 per cent of the global economy. The opportunity to strengthen economic cooperation with emerging powers such as India and China holds the promise of enhanced technology transfer and infrastructure financing and development, driving regional prosperity.

However, these potential benefits are tempered by significant challenges. If the four ASEAN countries gear towards membership, the BRICS partnership may risk fragmenting regional cohesion. Diverging priorities among ASEAN members could create rifts, undermining the organisation's collective strength. Furthermore, deeper ties with BRICS might strain existing relationships with Western partners, potentially decreasing foreign investment from those regions. Balancing interests between BRICS and Western economies will require careful navigation of geopolitical dynamics, as conflicting interests could arise.

Ultimately, the future of the AEC will hinge on how effectively ASEAN can manage these complexities while continuing to promote integration and cooperation across the region. The collective approach is vital for ASEAN to emerge as a cohesive economic entity that can leverage its strengths in a competitive global environment. ASEAN's economic integration journey has witnessed remarkable achievements, but as the global trade landscape evolves, ASEAN must adapt to new economic realities.

ASEAN can ensure that it remains competitive and integrated by modernising trade agreements, advancing its digital economy, and enhancing supply chain resilience. The opportunities are immense, with ASEAN positioned as a vibrant economic community ready to capitalise on the growing digital economy, regional trade partnerships, and the benefits of its strategic location. As ASEAN moves forward, balancing relationships with emerging economic blocs and global frameworks while fostering inclusive growth will be vital to achieving a sustainable and prosperous future.

Through these initiatives and collaborative efforts, ASEAN is securing its economic future and solidifying its role as a dynamic player on the global stage, prepared to steer the challenges and opportunities that lie ahead. The future is bright for ASEAN, with its commitment to integration, innovation, and resilience paving the way for a thriving economic community.

"ASEAN's economic future lies in deepening integration, expanding trade partnerships, and embracing innovation. As the region evolves, ASEAN must leverage its dynamic markets and

growing digital economy to stay competitive in the global landscape. ASEAN can ensure a prosperous and inclusive future for its member states by fostering innovation and sustainable growth."

Pushpanathan Sundram, Author

Chapter 9

Security Cooperation – Addressing Traditional & Non-Traditional Threats

"Intensify our efforts to promote sustainable security cooperation through strengthening capacities and cooperation amongst ASEAN Member States as well as with the Plus Countries in response to non-traditional and transnational security threats in the region in order to bring sustainable peace, stability and security to ASEAN."

Joint Declaration of the ASEAN Defence Ministers on Sustainable Security, July 2019

Since its establishment in 1967, ASEAN has continually adapted its security architecture to meet various challenges. Initially focused on fostering regional peace, ASEAN's mandate has significantly evolved to address an increasingly complex web of transnational issues that impact the region's stability. Traditional security concerns—border disputes and military conflicts—are now complemented by pressing non-traditional threats such as cybersecurity risks, climate change, public health emergencies, food insecurity, and antimicrobial resistance (AMR). This chapter will take you through ASEAN's proactive measures in managing these evolving threats. You will learn how the organisation employs multilateral cooperation and innovative policy frameworks to manage the intricacies of security in the 21st century. For instance, ASEAN's approach to cybersecurity emphasises collective capacity-building and sharing best practices among member states, which is crucial in an era where digital threats can undermine national security.

ASEAN has actively addressed climate change as a critical security concern, implementing strategic initiatives to build regional resilience and support sustainable development. The ASEAN Centre for Climate Change (ACCC) in Brunei Darussalam could be a central hub for coordinating climate action, providing policy recommendations, and fostering cooperation among member states. A robust climate finance strategy is essential to support these efforts, enabling member states to access necessary funds for priority projects in climate mitigation and adaptation alongside systems for monitoring, reporting, and verifying greenhouse gas emissions.

In the energy sector, projects like the Lao PDR-Thailand-Malaysia-Singapore Power Integration Project (LTMS-PIP) advance the integration of renewable energy through cross-border electricity trade, helping reduce the region's dependence on fossil fuels. Internationally, ASEAN regularly reinforces its commitment to climate action by issuing joint statements at UNFCCC sessions, advocating for increased support to developing countries. ASEAN must continue integrating climate resilience into its security policies, addressing current environmental challenges while preparing for future uncertainties.

Traditional security threats: balancing power with China

The South China Sea dispute is one of ASEAN's most pressing traditional security issues. This contentious situation remains a significant test for ASEAN's unity and diplomatic resolve. It is geopolitically vital and economically crucial, with over $3.8 trillion in trade passing through its waters each year. Moreover, the region is rich in resources, boasting 11 billion barrels of untapped oil and 190 trillion cubic feet of natural gas reserves. Consequently, overlapping territorial claims by China and four ASEAN member states—Vietnam, the Philippines, Malaysia, and Brunei—have escalated tensions.

China's assertion of the Nine-Dash Line has intensified these disputes, resulting in naval confrontations, militarisation of artificial islands, and violations of fishing rights. The 2016 Permanent Court of Arbitration (PCA) ruling invalidated China's claims based on the Nine-Dash Line, which was welcomed by ASEAN claimants like Vietnam and the Philippines but was summarily dismissed by China. ASEAN has sought to promote peaceful dialogue and adherence to a rules-based order in the South China Sea in response to this ongoing crisis. One step in the right direction was the Declaration on the Conduct of Parties in the South China Sea (DOC); the DOC, adopted in 2002, established a framework for confidence-building measures. However, the aspiration for a legally binding COC remains a work in progress as member states grapple with key issues related to militarisation, resource-sharing, and the essential principle of freedom of navigation.

In July of 2023, ASEAN and China convened in Jakarta to finalise the second draft of the COC. Yet, achieving consensus on critical issues such as resource extraction rights and the delineation of maritime boundaries continues to pose challenges. Countries like the Philippines and Vietnam advocate for stronger language to prevent unilateral actions, while Cambodia and Laos often align with China's interests. ASEAN aims to conclude the COC by 2025, offering a robust framework for dispute management and enhancing regional maritime stability.

In this respect, the ASEAN Defence Ministers' Meeting (ADMM) is pivotal in promoting military cooperation among member states. It has facilitated joint military exercises, strategic dialogues, and confidence-building initiatives. The ADMM-Plus expands military collaboration to include key dialogue partners such as the United States, China, Russia, Japan, South Korea, India, Australia, and New Zealand. In 2022, joint military exercises conducted by the ADMM-Plus focused on counterterrorism, maritime security, and humanitarian disaster relief. These exercises foster interoperability, strategic information sharing, and capacity-building among defence forces, equipping ASEAN with the collaborative tools necessary to address future security challenges.

Furthermore, the 1995 Treaty of SEANWFZ exemplifies ASEAN's commitment to maintaining a nuclear-free region. While the treaty prohibits nuclear weapons development, testing, and possession, its effectiveness relies on the participation of nuclear-armed states, including China, Russia, and the United States. Continued dialogue with these powers is crucial for achieving universal compliance with SEANWFZ and aligning regional security with global non-proliferation norms.

Non-traditional security threats

As the landscape of security threats evolves, ASEAN has recognised the pressing need to confront non-traditional threats through a multidimensional strategy. These threats include cybersecurity, public health, food security, climate change, and the rising challenge of AMR.

ASEAN's transnational crime fight: Strategies for a safer region

With ASEAN's digital economy projected to reach a remarkable $1 trillion by 2030, the rise of cyber threats has become a paramount concern. The frequency of cyberattacks in the region has surged by over 300% since

2020, targeting critical sectors such as finance, energy, and transportation. Southeast Asia's vulnerability stems from varying cybersecurity capacities, a rapidly growing digital user base, and inconsistent regulatory frameworks among member states. ASEAN has launched the ASEAN Cybersecurity Cooperation Strategy to enhance regional incident response capabilities and establish Cyber Emergency Response Teams (CERTs). The ASEAN-Singapore Cybersecurity Centre of Excellence (ASCCE), founded in 2019, has trained over 500 officials across ASEAN, bolstering regional cybersecurity resilience.

Looking to the future, ASEAN's cybersecurity priorities will focus on implementing cross-border data protection frameworks, fostering public-private partnerships to disseminate best practices, and integrating cybersecurity strategies with e-commerce and digital payment systems. By enhancing its digital infrastructure and fortifying cybersecurity measures, ASEAN aspires to build a trusted and secure digital ecosystem that supports its rapidly evolving economy.

ASEAN is actively addressing various other transnational crimes, including drug trafficking, human trafficking, and wildlife trafficking, through a series of strategic initiatives and collaborative efforts. Drug trafficking remains a critical challenge in the region, with Southeast Asia identified as one of the largest producers of methamphetamine globally. The United Nations Office on Drugs and Crime (UNODC) reported nearly 300 million methamphetamine tablets seized in the region in

2020, highlighting the scale of the issue. In response, ASEAN has implemented the ASEAN Work Plan on Securing Communities Against Illicit Drugs 2016-2025, which focuses on enhancing law enforcement cooperation, promoting public awareness campaigns, and strengthening regional capacities to combat drug-related crimes. This comprehensive approach aims not only to disrupt drug trafficking networks but also to address the underlying socio-economic factors contributing to drug abuse.

In addition to drug trafficking, human trafficking is a pressing concern for ASEAN, with the region being a significant source and destination for trafficked women and children. The UNODC estimates that Southeast Asia has approximately 1.5 million victims of human trafficking, driven by socio-economic disparities and demand for cheap labour and sexual exploitation. To combat this, ASEAN adopted the ASEAN Plan of Action to Combat Trafficking in Persons, emphasising regional cooperation, victim protection, and the enhancement of law enforcement capacities. This plan encourages member states to develop comprehensive national frameworks aligned with international standards to ensure a consistent regional approach.

Similarly, wildlife trafficking poses a significant threat. Southeast Asia serves as a central transit hub for illegal wildlife trade, which impacts endangered species such as elephants and tigers. The Action Plan aims to strengthen legal frameworks, promote public awareness, and enhance collaboration among member states to combat this growing threat effectively.

Through these initiatives, ASEAN demonstrates its commitment to a coordinated response to transnational crimes, focusing on enhancing regional cooperation, protecting vulnerable populations, and preserving biodiversity. The collective efforts reflect an understanding that addressing these complex issues requires comprehensive strategies that engage various sectors and stakeholders in the region.

Food security and nutrition: safeguarding lives and livelihoods

Ensuring food security and nutrition is paramount for ASEAN's over 680 million inhabitants, as it directly influences social stability and sustainable development. The region's food systems are increasingly susceptible to climate change, natural disasters, and economic shocks, which can disrupt food production and affordability. ASEAN has implemented the ASEAN Integrated Food Security (AIFS) Framework and the Strategic Plan of Action on Food Security (SPA-FS) to address these challenges.

These initiatives aim to enhance agricultural productivity, strengthen supply chain resilience, and promote sustainable food systems. By 2030, ASEAN targets a 50% increase in rice yield productivity, ensuring that 95% of its population has access to nutritionally adequate diets. Member states prioritise innovative farming practices, smart agriculture, and sustainable aquaculture to bolster food security.

The COVID-19 pandemic exposed vulnerabilities in ASEAN's food supply chains, including labour shortages, distribution inefficiencies, and export restrictions, underscoring the need for robust regional coordination. In response, ASEAN has reinforced its efforts through the ASEAN Food Security Reserve Board (AFSRB), focusing on securing food stockpiles and facilitating trade in essential goods during crises. For instance, the AFSRB manages the ASEAN Plus Three Emergency Rice Reserve (APTERR), which ensures rice availability during emergencies.

As ASEAN progresses, fostering resilience in food systems requires enhancing agricultural productivity and addressing social determinants of food security to ensure equitable access to nutritious food across all demographics. This includes implementing social protection measures, improving infrastructure, and promoting education on nutrition. Community collaboration among member states, private sectors, and international organisations is essential to build a sustainable and resilient regional food system.

Public health security: lessons from the pandemic

The COVID-19 pandemic underscored the need for robust public health systems and effective cross-border disease surveillance within ASEAN. In response, the establishment of the ASEAN Centre for Public Health Emergencies and Emerging Diseases (ACPHEED) was announced during the 37th ASEAN Summit on 12 November 2020. ACPHEED aims to enhance the region's capacity to prepare for, prevent, detect, and respond to public health emergencies and emerging diseases.

ASEAN created the COVID-19 ASEAN Response Fund to support immediate needs during the pandemic. This pool of financial resources helps member states detect, control, and prevent the transmission of COVID-19. The fund facilitates the procurement of necessary medical supplies and equipment, including test kits, personal protective equipment (PPE), and vaccines, ensuring equitable access across the region.

Building resilience in ASEAN's health supply chains is vital for future preparedness. The disruptions caused by COVID-19 highlighted the need for a more integrated and sustainable approach to health security. Key to this is the adoption of a One-Health approach, which recognises the interconnectedness of human, animal, and environmental health. By addressing issues such as zoonotic diseases and antimicrobial resistance (AMR), ASEAN can better prepare for emerging health threats that transcend national borders and sectors.

Fostering collaboration across governments, private sectors, and multilateral organisations is essential for tackling these challenges. Strengthened partnerships will enable ASEAN to mobilise resources, implement innovative solutions, and enhance regional capacity for surveillance and response. Lessons from the pandemic have laid a strong foundation for a more coordinated and resilient ASEAN health system, ready to address future crises with agility and inclusiveness.

Antimicrobial resistance: a silent crisis

It might come as a surprise to outsiders, but antimicrobial resistance (AMR) poses a significant public health threat in Southeast Asia, with over 500,000 deaths annually attributed to antibiotic-resistant infections. This alarming statistic reflects a broader global crisis where the misuse and overuse of antibiotics in human medicine, agriculture, and livestock production have contributed to the emergence of resistant pathogens.

According to a report from the World Health Organisation (WHO), inappropriate prescribing practices in healthcare settings, coupled with the excessive use of antibiotics in agriculture for growth promotion and disease prevention, have played pivotal roles in the rise of resistance. Studies have shown that approximately 70% of antibiotics sold globally are used in animals, which raises concerns about their potential to cause resistance that can subsequently affect human health. In particular, the use of antibiotics in livestock can lead to resistant zoonotic bacteria that can be transmitted to humans through the food chain, complicating the treatment of common infections.

In response to this pressing issue, ASEAN has implemented a comprehensive One Health approach that brings together experts from human health, animal health, and environmental sectors to develop a unified strategy against AMR. The ASEAN Strategic Framework to Combat Antimicrobial Resistance through One Health Approach (2019-2030) outlines critical priorities to combat this threat effectively. Among these priorities is regulating antibiotic use in agriculture, which involves creating guidelines and enforcing regulations to limit the indiscriminate use of antibiotics in livestock production. By ensuring that antibiotics are only used when necessary and under strict veterinary supervision, ASEAN aims to curb the rise of resistant pathogens.

Moreover, enhancing surveillance networks is a vital component of ASEAN's strategy. Improved data collection on antibiotic use and resistance patterns across member states will enable a better understanding of the AMR landscape, facilitating targeted interventions. This coordinated effort is essential, as projections indicate that AMR could lead to 10 million deaths globally by 2050, with Southeast Asia facing a substantial economic burden due to increased healthcare costs and lost productivity. By prioritising these strategies, ASEAN aims to mitigate the immediate threats AMR poses and safeguard public health and food security for future generations.

Climate change: a growing threat

Climate change represents one of ASEAN's most pressing non-traditional security challenges, with far-reaching implications for food security, public health, and regional stability. The region is particularly vulnerable to the impacts of climate change, including the increasing frequency of extreme weather events, rising sea levels, and shifting agricultural productivity patterns. These challenges not only threaten lives but also disrupt economic growth and livelihoods, making climate resilience a critical priority for ASEAN.

In response, ASEAN has established frameworks such as the ASEAN Agreement on Disaster Management and Emergency Response (AADMER) and the ASEAN Disaster Emergency Response Plan, which facilitate regional cooperation in tackling climate-related disasters. AADMER, for instance, provides a legal framework for coordinated disaster risk reduction and response efforts across member states. These initiatives emphasise the development of early warning systems, enhanced preparedness measures, and rapid response capabilities. Notable successes include the operationalisation of the ASEAN Coordinating Centre for Humanitarian Assistance on Disaster Management (AHA Centre), which has played a crucial role in responding to disasters like Typhoon Haiyan in the Philippines.

Looking ahead, ASEAN must prioritise climate adaptation and resilience-building strategies to safeguard its future. Investments in sustainable infrastructure—such as climate-resilient transport systems and flood mitigation projects—are vital. Besides, promoting environmentally friendly practices, including renewable energy adoption and sustainable agriculture, is essential for reducing greenhouse gas emissions and fostering long-term sustainability.

ASEAN must integrate climate change considerations into national policies and regional cooperation frameworks to strengthen its response. Collaborative efforts, such as the ASEAN Climate Change Initiative (ACCI), can enhance knowledge sharing and resource mobilisation, enabling member states to tackle this existential threat collectively. By adopting a unified approach to climate action, ASEAN can bolster its resilience and ensure a sustainable and secure future for the region.

Multilateral security cooperation

Through multilateral forums like the EAS and ARF, ASEAN's security architecture plays a focal role in enhancing security cooperation across the Indo-Pacific. These platforms provide essential opportunities for dialogue and collaboration among member states and key global powers, addressing traditional and non-traditional security challenges.

The EAS convenes annually to tackle strategic security, political, and economic issues impacting the region. Its inclusive format allows ASEAN to engage with major powers, including the United States, China, India, and Japan, on various matters, from counterterrorism to nuclear non-proliferation. For instance, in the EAS held in 2021, discussions included cybersecurity threats and climate change impacts on security, reflecting ASEAN's commitment to broadening its security agenda. The EAS Leaders' Statement on Cybersecurity Cooperation emphasises the need for enhanced collaboration to combat cyber threats and promote a secure digital environment.

The ARF remains a central platform for ASEAN-led security dialogue, emphasising preventive diplomacy and confidence-building measures. As Asia-Pacific's first and largest regional security forum, the ARF has been instrumental in promoting cooperation on maritime disputes and security. The ARF Work Plan on Maritime Security, endorsed in 2021, outlines measures to combat illegal fishing, enhance joint maritime patrols, and promote freedom of navigation. One notable example of this cooperation is the ARF's involvement in the ASEAN Maritime Forum, which has facilitated dialogues on issues such as search and rescue operations and the management of maritime disputes in the South China Sea.

In 2020, the ARF held a series of virtual meetings addressing the impact of the COVID-19 pandemic on regional security, showcasing its adaptability and commitment to addressing emerging challenges. The forum's discussions led to the ARF Statement on Enhancing Cooperation in Responding to the COVID-19 Pandemic, which highlighted the importance of information sharing and collaboration among member states to strengthen health security. While these forums effectively address various security concerns, they also highlight the need for continuous engagement and adaptation to evolving threats. ASEAN's commitment to fostering dialogue and collaboration among its members and external partners is crucial for enhancing regional stability and addressing the complexities of security in the Indo-Pacific.

Balancing traditional and non-traditional security threats

ASEAN's dual approach to addressing traditional territorial disputes and non-traditional security threats is critical for ensuring comprehensive security in the region. This strategy balances national sovereignty with collective security interests, acknowledging the interconnectedness of various security issues and the necessity for collaborative responses. The Association's ongoing efforts to tackle transnational crimes, such as human trafficking and drug trafficking, highlight the need for coordinated action across member states. The ASEAN Plan of Action to Combat Trafficking in Persons (ACTIP) exemplifies this commitment, focusing on regional cooperation and victim protection to address the complexities of human trafficking effectively.

Combatting antimicrobial resistance (AMR) is becoming increasingly important within ASEAN's security framework, in addition to transnational crimes. The region faces significant public health threats from AMR, which is exacerbated by the misuse of antibiotics in human and veterinary practices. ASEAN's regional action plan on AMR emphasises a One Health approach that integrates efforts across human, animal, and environmental health sectors. By investing in public health initiatives and promoting responsible antibiotic use, ASEAN aims to safeguard the well-being of its diverse populations.

ASEAN recognises the importance of building resilient food systems and enhancing public health security to confront these multifaceted challenges. Investments in sustainable agriculture and innovative farming practices improve food security and contribute to economic stability. Strengthening public health security has proven essential, as demonstrated by ASEAN's coordinated response to the COVID-19 pandemic, which involved sharing information, resources, and best practices among member states. Cyber resilience is another critical area in which ASEAN focuses on protecting member states from evolving cyber threats through improved capabilities and comprehensive policies.

As ASEAN's security landscape evolves, the organisation must remain adaptable to these diverse threats. By promoting regional cooperation, prioritising innovation, and strengthening multilateral partnerships, ASEAN can develop a resilient security framework that ensures peace, prosperity, and stability in Southeast Asia. This proactive approach, commitment to inclusive security policies, and engagement with global partners are essential for addressing future challenges and securing ASEAN's future.

> *"ASEAN's political-security cooperation has expanded beyond traditional state sovereignty and territorial*

integrity concerns to address non-traditional security challenges such as climate change, cybersecurity, and transnational crime. By building a cohesive security framework, ASEAN strengthens regional stability, ensuring that both traditional and emerging threats are met with collective resilience."

Pushpanathan Sundram, Author

Chapter 10

Sustainable Development & Climate Action in ASEAN

Southeast Asia is one of the world's most vulnerable regions to the impacts of climate change, and the journey towards adopting climate-smart practices and achieving sustainable development is a continuous effort that demands collective diligence, unwavering commitment, and innovative approaches. ASEAN cooperation is important in charting a course towards a more resilient, adaptive, and sustainable ASEAN Community, guided by a shared vision of prosperity and environmental stewardship.

ASEAN Secretary-General Kao Kim Hourn, Opening Remarks at the Regional Workshop on Building Climate Smart ASEAN, Lao PDR, September 4, 2024

Southeast Asia stands at a crucial crossroads, confronted with pressing environmental challenges exacerbated by climate change. With over 680 million people living in a region characterised by rapid industrialisation and urbanisation, ASEAN countries face the formidable challenge of balancing economic growth with environmental sustainability. As a result, the urgency of sustainable development and climate action has become paramount. Adverse impacts of climate change—global warming, extreme weather events, and rising sea levels—threaten human security, disrupt economies, and endanger ecosystems.

The 2021 Global Climate Risk Index revealed ASEAN's vulnerability to climate change, ranking several ASEAN nations, including Myanmar, the Philippines, Thailand, Vietnam, and Cambodia, among those most affected by extreme weather occurrences. The Intergovernmental Panel on Climate Change (IPCC) predicts that temperatures in Southeast Asia will rise faster than the global average, increasing the frequency and intensity of climate-related disasters. Any conversation about ASEAN's future must include and clarify the efforts and necessity to achieve sustainability goals.

As a result, in this chapter, I will share with you ASEAN's various policies and frameworks for promoting sustainability and improving environmental resilience. The number of noteworthy activities in this direction is constantly growing; therefore, we'll focus on major developments like the AATHP and the ASEAN Action Plan on Climate Change. Furthermore, we will look at ASEAN's involvement in global environmental governance, its contributions to the Paris Agreement, and other international climate initiatives. ASEAN's commitment to sustainability demonstrates a shared ambition to create a more resilient future for the region.

Challenges of climate change

The impacts of climate change are becoming increasingly stark in Southeast Asia, a region characterised by diverse ecosystems and economic activities. The high frequency of natural disasters—such as typhoons, floods, droughts, and landslides—has become more severe and unpredictable. For instance, the devastating Typhoon Haiyan, known as Yolanda in the Philippines, struck the central Philippines on November 8, 2013, and remains one of the strongest tropical cyclones ever recorded. The storm caused widespread devastation, displacing approximately 4.1 million people and resulting in at least 6,300 confirmed fatalities. Economic damages were estimated at $2.98 billion.

Similarly, Thailand's annual floods disrupt lives and livelihoods, highlighting the nation's vulnerability to climate-induced disasters. According to the Asian Development Bank (ADB), the total economic losses from climate-related disasters in Southeast Asia could reach $6.7 trillion by 2100 if no preventive measures are undertaken.

Low-lying coastal areas, including bustling urban centres like Bangkok and Jakarta, face the dire threat of rising sea levels. According to the World Bank, projections indicate that by 2050, approximately 49 million people in East Asia and the Pacific could be internally displaced due to climate-related factors. The potential for displacement raises urgent questions about infrastructure resilience, urban planning, and the social implications of climate change, especially for the most vulnerable populations, including low-income communities and Indigenous groups.

Moreover, Southeast Asia's rich biodiversity is under siege. The region's forests, wetlands, and marine ecosystems are vital for their environmental functions and for supporting the livelihoods of millions. Deforestation, driven by logging, agriculture, and urban expansion, has led to significant habitat loss, impacting species diversity and disrupting ecological balance. The Food and Agriculture Organisation (FAO) estimates that Southeast Asia experienced a net loss of approximately 42 million hectares of forest between 1990 and 2005. This significant deforestation has adversely affected the region's biodiversity and carbon storage capacity, contributing to environmental degradation and climate change.

The Global Forest Watch indicates that Indonesia lost approximately 3.75 million hectares of tree cover in 2021, with 1.5 million hectares occurring within primary forests. While Indonesia has achieved a 25% reduction in the rate of primary forest loss, the situation is still concerning. Its impact threatens critical habitats and substantially contributes to greenhouse gas emissions, underscoring the urgent need for effective conservation strategies.

The degradation of marine habitats, particularly coral reefs, further threatens fish populations and the communities that depend on them for food and income. Coral reefs in Southeast Asia are experiencing significant bleaching events due to rising ocean temperatures and acidification. A study published in PLOS ONE indicates that between 1985 and 2017, approximately 71% of the world's coral reefs likely experienced bleaching at least once, with Southeast Asia among the most affected regions. This degradation poses a substantial threat to marine biodiversity and jeopardises the livelihoods of over 120 million people in the region who depend on these ecosystems for fishing and tourism.

Agricultural communities, especially in countries like Vietnam, Thailand, and the Philippines, are acutely aware of climate change's threats to food security. Unpredictable weather patterns have reduced agricultural productivity, affecting key crops such as rice, palm oil, and coffee. The consequences ripple through rural economies, threatening livelihoods and food availability. For instance, Vietnam's Mekong Delta, a critical rice-growing area, faces rising salinity and flooding, endangering the country's status as a leading rice exporter. The World Bank estimates that climate change could reduce agricultural productivity in the region by 10% to 30% by 2050, leading to significant food insecurity and economic instability.

The rapid pace of urbanisation and industrialisation also exacerbates environmental degradation. As cities expand, emissions of greenhouse gases (GHGs) increase, alongside the loss of natural habitats. The region's heavy reliance on coal and other fossil fuels for energy only intensifies its carbon footprint, making Southeast Asia one of the highest contributors to global emissions.

ASEAN nations collectively contribute approximately 5.4% of global carbon dioxide (CO_2) emissions. In 2022, Indonesia alone accounted for about 729 million metric tons of CO_2 emissions, making it one of the top emitters in the Asia-Pacific region. Urban centres like Manila and Ho Chi Minh City face significant challenges related to waste management, air pollution, and access to clean water, which pose substantial public health risks. In Ho Chi Minh City, rapid urbanisation has strained water resources, leading to issues such as surface water pollution and inadequate clean water provision for urban dwellers.

Additionally, the city's solid waste management system has been under pressure. A large proportion of waste is recyclable but not fully utilised due to the absence of a selective collection system. Furthermore, the World Health Organisation (WHO) estimates that air pollution is responsible for approximately 4.2 million deaths globally each year, with a substantial portion occurring in Southeast Asia due to urbanisation and industrial activities.

Addressing these environmental and public health challenges requires comprehensive strategies, including improving waste management infrastructure, enhancing air quality monitoring, and ensuring equitable access to clean water. Such measures are essential for promoting sustainable urban development and safeguarding public health in these rapidly growing cities.

Agriculture and greenhouse gas emissions

Each year, climate change causes Southeast Asian people to lose billions of dollars and hundreds of lives, but the causes of carbon emissions are manifold. The agricultural sector significantly contributes to GHG emissions in Southeast Asia. According to the ADB, Asia alone accounts for 43.2% of global emissions originating from agricultural activities.

Rice cultivation and livestock production are particularly noteworthy causes of these emissions. Flooded rice paddies are a source of methane (CH_4), a potent greenhouse gas with a global warming potential over 25 times that of carbon dioxide (CO_2) over 100 years. Globally, rice cultivation accounts for approximately 13% of agricultural methane emissions. In Southeast Asia, the activity is a major GHG contributor, with an average of 20% of emissions at the country level.

The main drivers of these emissions include poor water management, prolonged flooding, and the use of fertilisers. Farmers using traditional practices may inadvertently create anaerobic conditions conducive to methane production. Initiatives promoting water-saving techniques, such as alternate wetting and drying (AWD), can significantly reduce methane emissions. Studies have shown that AWD can reduce methane emissions by 30-50%, showcasing a potential pathway for mitigating climate impacts while maintaining rice productivity.

Livestock, particularly cattle, is another primary source of GHG emissions in ASEAN. Livestock farming emits methane through enteric fermentation, a digestive process in ruminant animals. According to the Food and Agriculture Organisation (FAO), livestock production is a significant source of methane emissions, contributing approximately 44% of global anthropogenic methane emissions. This substantial contribution underscores the importance of implementing sustainable livestock management practices to mitigate greenhouse gas emissions and address climate change challenges.

In ASEAN countries like Indonesia, Thailand, and Vietnam, the increasing demand for meat and dairy products has increased livestock production, further intensifying emissions. Sustainable livestock management practices can mitigate these emissions, including improved feeding strategies, manure management, and breeding programs for higher feed efficiency. For example, integrating forage crops into livestock diets can enhance digestion efficiency and reduce methane emissions, showcasing improved livestock productivity and lower environmental impact.

So, what does ASEAN do about it?

ASEAN has recognised the urgent need to address climate change and promote sustainable development through comprehensive frameworks designed to enhance resilience and environmental sustainability. These frameworks align closely with global sustainability goals, including the UN SDGs, particularly SDG 13, which emphasises climate action.

The ASCC Blueprint 2025 outlines a vision for environmental sustainability and climate adaptation, underscoring the Association's commitment to mitigating climate change impacts and promoting sustainable energy practices. The blueprint identifies several priorities: enhancing disaster risk reduction mechanisms, encouraging sustainable consumption and production practices, and strengthening adaptation strategies to bolster the resilience of vulnerable communities. For example, ASEAN has initiated regional efforts to improve disaster preparedness and response through the AADMER, which facilitates cooperation and coordination among member states during disasters.

Furthermore, the ASEAN Framework on Climate Change (AFCC) emphasises mitigation and adaptation strategies tailored to each member state's unique needs. This framework promotes regional collaboration and knowledge sharing, ensuring all ASEAN countries can access best practices and innovative solutions. Recent initiatives include the establishment of the ACCI, which focuses on enhancing regional capacities to address climate-related challenges. This initiative supports capacity-building efforts, technology transfer, and investment in climate-resilient infrastructure.

ASEAN actively partners with external entities to enhance its climate action efforts. For instance, ASEAN collaborates with international organisations such as the United Nations Development Programme (UNDP) and the Global Environment Facility (GEF) to implement projects to increase climate resilience and sustainability. These projects often focus on critical areas such as renewable energy development, sustainable land management, and community-based adaptation initiatives.

ASEAN is committed to sustainable development and climate action through its comprehensive frameworks and collaborative initiatives. By aligning its strategies with global goals and fostering cooperation among member states and international partners, ASEAN aims to create a resilient and sustainable future for Southeast Asia.

Transboundary haze pollution

One of ASEAN's notable agreements is the ASEAN Agreement on Transboundary Haze Pollution (AATHP), adopted in 2002 to address the recurrent haze pollution stemming from forest fires, primarily in Indonesia. This environmental issue has far-reaching consequences, impacting public health and regional economies in Malaysia, Singapore, and Brunei. Under this agreement, member states are committed to collaborating to prevent and mitigate haze pollution, focusing on sustainable land management practices and enhancing regional disaster response capabilities.

According to the ASEAN Secretariat, haze pollution challenges persist despite progress, with significant economic costs estimated at $9 billion annually due to health impacts and lost productivity. The economic burden includes healthcare costs, decreased agricultural productivity, and damage to tourism. Efforts to refine monitoring systems and early warning mechanisms are continually being developed to address these persistent challenges. Establishing the ASEAN Haze Monitoring System is crucial in improving regional cooperation and response to air quality issues.

The agreement has spurred initiatives to improve sustainable agricultural practices and land management. Countries like Indonesia have begun implementing measures to reduce peatland degradation, a significant contributor to haze pollution. By promoting sustainable palm oil production and reforestation efforts, Indonesia aims to mitigate future haze events while fostering economic development.

ASEAN action plan on climate change

The ASEAN Climate Strategic Action Plan (ACCSAP) is a strategic framework for tackling climate change through mitigation, adaptation, and climate financing efforts. Mitigation measures include commitments from member states to reduce carbon emissions by promoting renewable energy sources, improving energy efficiency, and embracing clean technologies. Countries like Vietnam and Thailand have made substantial advancements in developing solar and wind energy capacity as part of their low-carbon economy strategies. For instance, Vietnam aims for renewable energy to comprise 30% of its total energy mix by 2030, with plans to increase solar power capacity to 20,000 MW.

Adaptation initiatives focus on increasing resilience in agriculture, fisheries, and coastal management, developing climate-resilient infrastructure, and enhancing disaster preparedness. Integrating climate financing is critical to supporting these initiatives, and ASEAN aims to mobilise public and private funding to finance necessary climate actions. Of note, the ASEAN Green Bond Standards serve as a framework to guide investments in sustainable projects, facilitating the flow of capital into green initiatives.

In recent years, ASEAN has increased its focus on climate finance to support adaptation and mitigation efforts. The ASEAN Catalytic Green Finance Facility (ACGF), an initiative under the ASEAN Infrastructure Fund, was launched in April 2019 to accelerate green infrastructure investments in Southeast Asia. The ACGF provides technical assistance to ASEAN member governments and access to over $1 billion in loans from co-financing partners. This initiative aims to mobilise resources for climate-resilient infrastructure projects, supporting the region's transition to a sustainable, low-carbon economy.

Promoting green growth and renewable energy

Promoting green growth, which fosters economic development while minimising environmental degradation, is central to ASEAN's sustainability agenda. Transitioning to a green economy is reflected in efforts to advance renewable energy, improve energy efficiency, and adopt sustainable practices across key sectors.

The ASEAN Plan of Action for Energy Cooperation (APAEC) outlines regional cooperation in the energy sector, emphasising the promotion of renewable energy and energy efficiency. The APAEC 2016-2025 targets a 23% share of primary energy from renewable sources by 2025. As of 2023, ASEAN has achieved approximately 14% renewable energy consumption, primarily driven by investments in solar, wind, and hydropower projects. For instance, Vietnam has emerged as a leader in solar power installations, boasting over 18,500 MW of solar capacity installed by the end of 2022. The country is expected to continue expanding its solar power initiatives, driven by favourable government policies and investment incentives.

Laos and Thailand have made significant investments in hydropower, with Laos planning to export excess energy to neighbouring countries. Indonesia is expanding its geothermal capacity, accounting for 40% of the world's total geothermal energy. As of 2022, the country has achieved an installed geothermal capacity of 2,356 megawatts (MW), ranking second globally after the United States.

In addition to the energy sector, the agriculture and fisheries industries are critical to the ASEAN economy. Yet, they are highly vulnerable to environmental degradation and climate change impacts. The Strategic Plan of Action (SPA) for ASEAN Cooperation on Food,

Agriculture, and Forestry seeks to promote sustainable agricultural practices, reduce farming's environmental footprint, and improve fisheries management. This plan emphasises organic farming, sustainable land management to safeguard soil health and biodiversity, and sustainable fishing practices that protect marine ecosystems.

Integrating sustainable practices is vital for preserving the natural resources upon which millions in the region depend. For example, ASEAN countries have committed to reducing food waste as part of the ASEAN Guidelines and Action Plan for Sustainable Agriculture and Food Systems, aligning their agricultural policies with the UN SDGs. This commitment involves enhancing food supply chain management, promoting sustainable agricultural techniques, and encouraging responsible consumer consumption patterns.

In response to climate change's impacts on agriculture, ASEAN is also investing in research and development to promote climate-resilient crop varieties. This includes developing seeds that withstand extreme weather conditions, pests, and diseases. Collaborative efforts between governments, research institutions, and the private sector are essential to driving innovation and disseminating knowledge among farmers.

ASEAN's role in global climate governance

Due to its high vulnerability to climate change, Southeast Asia has emerged as an active participant in global climate governance. ASEAN member states have aligned their policies with international frameworks such as the Paris Agreement, which seeks to limit global temperature rise to below 2°C, ideally below 1.5°C. Each ASEAN member state has submitted its Nationally Determined Contributions (NDCs) detailing commitments to reduce greenhouse gas emissions, emphasising renewable energy production, enhancing climate adaptation, and mobilising climate financing.

ASEAN's involvement in global climate governance includes collaboration with international partners, such as the European Union, the United Nations Framework Convention on Climate Change (UNFCCC), and the Global Green Growth Institute (GGGI). These partnerships facilitate knowledge sharing, capacity building, and the implementation of climate policies. Furthermore, ASEAN has actively participated in global climate summits, including the COP meetings, advocating for the interests of developing countries in the region. Establishing the ASEAN Working Group on Climate Change (AWGCC) is a testament to the region's commitment to addressing climate issues collectively. This working group focuses on developing regional strategies to implement the Paris Agreement and enhance cooperation among member states.

Disaster risk reduction is a critical component of ASEAN's adaptation strategy. Significant progress has been made through partnerships with entities like the United Nations Office for Disaster Risk Reduction

(UNDRR) and the World Bank. The AADMER is a cornerstone of the regional disaster risk reduction framework, and the AHA Centre plays a vital role in coordinating disaster response and sharing best practices.

In 2023, ASEAN member states collectively committed to integrating disaster risk reduction into national development planning, enhancing regional preparedness for natural disasters, and improving resilience to climate impacts. This includes investments in early warning systems, public awareness campaigns, and community-based disaster risk management approaches, ensuring that vulnerable populations are equipped to cope with climate-related challenges.

Role of carbon trading in ASEAN

You may not have heard of carbon trading yet, but let me explain: it's essentially a system designed to tackle climate change by turning pollution into a commodity. Think of it as a marketplace where companies can buy and sell the right to emit carbon dioxide (or other greenhouse gases).

Here's how it works: governments or international bodies set a limit, called a "cap," on the total amount of emissions allowed. Companies are given or can purchase permits to emit a specific amount. If a company manages to reduce its emissions and has leftover permits, it can sell them to another company that needs more. This creates two significant incentives: a) Companies that reduce emissions can profit by selling their permits, and b)

Companies that pollute more have to pay for it, making pollution costly.

An interesting approach to managing carbon emissions involves two fundamental mechanisms: Cap-and-Trade and Carbon Offsets. Under a Cap-and-Trade system, the government imposes a cap on total pollution levels, allocating permits to companies for a set amount of emissions. Businesses that exceed their limits must purchase additional permits from those that emit less, fostering a market where reducing pollution becomes financially advantageous. Complementing this is the concept of Carbon Offsets, where companies can invest in projects that actively remove carbon from the atmosphere, such as reforestation or renewable energy initiatives. By participating in these systems, businesses not only comply with regulations but also contribute to broader environmental goals, turning sustainability into a practical and impactful endeavour.

Carbon trading turns the fight against climate change into a collaborative and market-driven process, encouraging businesses to innovate and cut emissions efficiently. ASEAN is actively exploring carbon trading mechanisms to reduce emissions and promote sustainable practices as part of its climate change mitigation strategies. Carbon trading allows countries to buy and sell carbon credits, providing financial incentives for reducing greenhouse gas emissions.

Carbon trading has several potential benefits for ASEAN countries. It can encourage investments in clean energy and sustainable technologies, creating new economic opportunities. ASEAN nations can access international funding for renewable energy projects and climate adaptation initiatives by participating in carbon markets. This financial support can accelerate the transition to low-carbon economies and enhance resilience to climate impacts. Moreover, carbon trading can foster regional cooperation among ASEAN member states. By establishing a regional carbon market, countries can collaborate on emissions reduction targets, share best practices, and enhance monitoring and reporting systems. This collaboration can lead to more effective climate action and a stronger collective response to climate change challenges.

Indonesia and Thailand have taken steps toward developing domestic carbon trading systems. Indonesia, for instance, is piloting a carbon trading scheme in its forestry sector, aiming to leverage carbon credits from forest conservation and reforestation efforts. Meanwhile, Thailand is exploring options for implementing a national emissions trading system as part of its commitment to reducing emissions under its NDCs.

However, implementing carbon trading mechanisms also faces challenges. The effectiveness of carbon markets relies on robust regulatory frameworks, transparent monitoring systems, and credible accounting of emissions reductions. Moreover, ensuring that carbon trading mechanisms benefit local communities and vulnerable populations is crucial to avoid exacerbating social inequalities.

Transitioning to a circular economy

The transition to a circular economy represents a vital step for ASEAN as it seeks to minimise resource consumption and mitigate environmental impact while fostering sustainable economic growth. A circular economy aims to create a closed-loop system where waste is minimised, resources are reused and recycled, and products are designed for durability and sustainability. This model is particularly crucial for Southeast Asia, a region experiencing rapid urbanisation and industrialisation, which has led to significant waste generation and environmental degradation.

In the ASEAN context, the circular economy integrates principles of sustainable development into economic activities, thereby promoting resource efficiency and environmental stewardship. Shifting from a linear economy, characterised by resource extraction, use, and disposal, to a circular economy is especially relevant in Southeast Asia, where rapid growth often exacerbates existing environmental challenges.

The Framework for Circular Economy for the ASEAN Economic Community, adopted in 2021, serves as a guiding document for member states to implement circular economy practices. This framework encourages the adoption of policies that promote recycling, sustainable consumption, and resource efficiency across various sectors, including agriculture, manufacturing, and waste management. By fostering a circular economy, ASEAN aims to enhance its competitiveness while reducing environmental impacts and addressing pressing challenges such as climate change and resource scarcity.

Central to the transition to a circular economy is the implementation of effective waste management strategies, which are fundamental to minimising environmental impact. ASEAN member states can benefit from developing comprehensive waste management systems that prioritise reduction, recycling, and recovery. Countries like Singapore have set an exemplary standard with their Zero Waste Masterplan, aiming to divert at least 70% of waste from landfills by 2030 through recycling and resource recovery initiatives. This approach minimises waste and fosters a culture of sustainability and responsible consumption among the population.

Moreover, encouraging sustainable product design is crucial for promoting a circular economy. ASEAN can promote policies that incentivise manufacturers to create products that boast longer lifespans, modular designs for easy repair, and materials that are recyclable or biodegradable. By integrating eco-design principles, companies can reduce waste at the source and enhance resource efficiency. Collaborative efforts between governments, businesses, and design experts are essential to develop guidelines that facilitate circular product development. This contributes to waste reduction and spurs innovation within industries, creating new business models centred on sustainability.

The success of a circular economy in ASEAN also relies heavily on changing consumer behaviour. A shift in consumer mindset is vital for a circular economy to thrive, and this can be achieved through awareness campaigns that educate consumers about the benefits of sustainable consumption. Such initiatives can highlight the importance of choosing eco-friendly products, reducing reliance on single-use items, and understanding the lifecycle of the products they purchase. Implementing labelling systems that indicate the recyclability or sustainability of products can further guide consumers in making informed choices.

In addition to these strategies, leveraging technology is critical to advancing circular economy initiatives within the region. Innovations in recycling technologies, waste-to-energy systems, and digital platforms for resource sharing can facilitate the transition. For example, ASEAN countries can invest in Internet of Things (IoT) solutions that enhance waste management efficiency by providing real-time data on waste generation and recycling rates. Embracing technology improves operational efficiency and cultivates a culture of innovation that supports sustainable practices.

Furthermore, the successful implementation of a circular economy requires collaboration across sectors and borders. ASEAN can facilitate partnerships between governments, private companies, civil society, and academic institutions to share best practices, resources, and technologies. Regional initiatives, such as the ASEAN Circular Economy Network, can provide a platform for stakeholders to collaborate on circular economy projects, enabling knowledge exchange and fostering innovation. By working together, ASEAN member states can create synergies that enhance the effectiveness of circular economy initiatives.

Transitioning to a circular economy offers significant economic benefits for ASEAN. By reducing resource consumption and waste, member states can lower production costs, enhance competitiveness, and create new job opportunities in recycling and sustainable manufacturing sectors. This model addresses environmental concerns and strengthens economic resilience against fluctuations in resource prices or disruptions in supply chains, promoting local sourcing and resource efficiency. Moreover, the circular economy aligns with ASEAN's broader sustainability goals, including commitments to the UN SDGs. By prioritising resource efficiency, waste reduction, and sustainable consumption, ASEAN can significantly contribute to achieving SDG 12: Responsible Consumption and Production, which emphasises the importance of sustainable practices in ensuring long-term economic growth.

ASEAN's journey toward sustainability is multifaceted, reflecting a commitment to addressing climate change, promoting renewable energy, and embracing sustainable development practices. While the challenges are significant, ASEAN's resolve to pursue green growth, resilience, and global cooperation underscores its determination to combat environmental degradation. By emphasising collaboration, innovation, and effective policy implementation, ASEAN is well-positioned to contribute to global sustainability efforts and pave the way for a greener, more equitable future for the region. The success of these initiatives relies on strong political will and the active engagement of civil society, private sector stakeholders, and local communities in achieving sustainable outcomes.

The path ahead will require ASEAN to remain adaptable and responsive to the evolving climate landscape, leveraging technology, international cooperation, and grassroots movements to foster a sustainable future. As the region moves forward, the commitment to building a resilient ASEAN Community will be paramount, ensuring that future generations inherit a thriving, sustainable environment.

Asia Zero Emission Community and ASEAN collaboration

The Asia Zero Emission Community (AZEC) represents a significant advancement in regional cooperation among ASEAN member states and their partners, aiming to accelerate the transition towards carbon neutrality. Established during the 2nd AZEC Leaders Meeting in October 2024, this initiative brings together countries like

Australia, Japan, and all ASEAN nations, except Myanmar, to collectively address the urgent challenges posed by climate change. Leaders reaffirmed their commitment to deep, rapid, and sustained reductions in greenhouse gas emissions, emphasising the need for collaborative action in line with the Paris Agreement and global climate conference outcomes, such as COP28.

Central to AZEC's framework is the operationalisation of the Asia Zero Emission Centre, which serves as a hub for sharing knowledge and best practices and developing tailored decarbonisation strategies for each member country. This centre facilitates the exchange of information on renewable energy technologies and helps member states create actionable roadmaps to achieve their carbon neutrality goals. By emphasising the principles of "one goal, various pathways," AZEC acknowledges the unique circumstances of each country while promoting inclusive economic growth and energy security.

ASEAN can work with the AZEC to enhance collaboration among member states and external partners in addressing climate change and promoting sustainable development. By aligning its initiatives with global climate goals, ASEAN can effectively mobilise resources and expertise from various stakeholders, including international organisations, the private sector, and research institutions. Collaborations with entities such as the International Energy Agency (IEA) and the Global Environment Facility (GEF) can provide technical assistance and funding for renewable energy projects and capacity-building initiatives. Furthermore, establishing regional frameworks for sharing best practices through initiatives like the ASEAN Centre for Energy (ACE) will drive innovation and create robust responses to climate challenges.

Leveraging the AZEC Centre as a research and development hub will enable ASEAN to stay ahead of emerging technologies and market trends in the clean energy sector. This centre can facilitate collaborative research projects, pilot programs, and training sessions on decarbonisation and sustainable practices. By fostering a culture of collaboration and knowledge-sharing among its member states and partners, ASEAN can build a comprehensive strategy to address current and future climate challenges, ensuring Southeast Asia's sustainable and resilient future.

Future directions for ASEAN's sustainability agenda

The path toward sustainable development and climate action in ASEAN is complex but crucial. The region's commitment to addressing climate change, promoting renewable energy, and adopting sustainable practices is evident in initiatives like the AZEC, which unites ASEAN member countries with partners such as Australia and Japan to accelerate the transition to carbon neutrality. By emphasising shared goals for reducing greenhouse gas emissions and promoting renewable energy technologies, ASEAN aims to align its economic policies with global sustainability objectives, particularly those outlined in UN SDGs.

Critical priorities for ASEAN include expanding climate resilience through investments in climate-resistant infrastructure, which is vital for mitigating the impacts of extreme weather events. This involves developing flood defences, enhancing transportation networks, and improving water management systems. For instance, the construction of resilient drainage systems and seawalls is essential for urban areas prone to flooding, particularly as climate change leads to more frequent and intense weather patterns. By investing in sustainable urban planning initiatives and green infrastructure, ASEAN can significantly reduce vulnerability to climate-related disasters, protecting communities and ecosystems.

Moreover, community engagement and education play crucial roles in fostering climate resilience. Empowering local communities with knowledge and resources to adapt to climate change is essential for building a sustainable future. Educational programs focusing on climate awareness, sustainable agricultural practices, and disaster preparedness can significantly enhance community resilience. Programs such as the ACCI facilitate the sharing of best practices and innovative solutions across member states, ensuring that local populations are equipped to face environmental challenges. Promoting community-based adaptation strategies, including participatory planning processes, can strengthen local capacities to respond to climate impacts. By integrating these approaches and fostering a culture of sustainability, ASEAN is poised to build a robust framework for climate action and sustainable development that addresses current challenges and prepares for future uncertainties.

> *"Sustainable development and climate action are at the core of ASEAN's long-term vision. ASEAN can safeguard its environment and build resilient economies and societies by aligning regional efforts with global sustainability goals. ASEAN's commitment to sustainability is critical to ensuring that future generations can thrive in a stable and productive region."*
>
> **Pushpanathan Sundram, Author**

Chapter 11

ASEAN's Global Engagement – Expanding ASEAN's Role in International Affairs

"Many Asian countries recognise the importance of all the major powers having stakes in and contributing to the region's stability and development. Hence, ASEAN, the Southeast Asian countries has long sought to build a dense web of cooperation, interdependence, and having overlapping circles of friends."

Prime Minister Lee Hsien Loong at the closing dialogue for the Asia Future Summit 2023, Singapore October 5, 2023

ASEAN's diplomatic journey, initially rooted in regional cooperation, has matured over the last four decades, witnessing robust dialogue partnerships, impactful FTAs, and active participation in multilateral arrangements. Imagine ASEAN as a diplomatic bridge, connecting Southeast Asia with major global players and serving as a crucial voice in the Asia-Pacific and beyond. As we explore this chapter, we must recognise the profound shifts in the global landscape. Changes in geopolitical power, evolving trade dynamics, and pressing issues like climate change and security challenges have redefined how countries interact. ASEAN's adaptability in responding to these changes has solidified its role in global governance. We will discover how ASEAN has enhanced its international engagement, fostering partnerships with influential powers and international organisations to address the challenges of our time. This chapter attempts to uncover the intricacies of ASEAN's external relations and its strategic importance in the contemporary world.

ASEAN's external relations

ASEAN's 11 dialogue partners are a vital component of its worldwide engagement strategy, helping the organisation to broaden its diplomatic and economic reach. These collaborations are essential platforms for advancing ASEAN's strategic interests on a global scale. ASEAN has effectively negotiated a complicated web of geopolitical interests by fostering regional peace, stability, and growth.

The development of Comprehensive Strategic Partnerships (CSPs) has marked a significant shift in ASEAN's external relations, emphasising the organisation's strategic role in the Asia Pacific region. These collaborations strengthen ASEAN's influence and promote closer cooperation in various areas, including security, trade, infrastructure, and sustainable development. The ASEAN-China CSP, launched in 2021, symbolises ASEAN and China's expanding connections, with China serving as ASEAN's major trading partner. Two-way trade was nearly $722 billion in 2022, reflecting the significant economic interconnectedness that has developed over time. The ACFTA, which has been in place since 2010, has aided this expansion by allowing for more efficient trade flows in products, services, and investments. Furthermore, China's Belt and Road Initiative (BRI) is critical to accelerating ASEAN infrastructure development. Major BRI projects, such as trains, ports, and energy infrastructure, improve regional connections and promote economic growth.

Chinese investments in ASEAN infrastructure have surpassed $40 billion in the past decade, cementing its position as a key economic partner. FDI from China into ASEAN was approximately $15.5 billion in 2022, further highlighting the depth of economic ties. Politically, China remains actively engaged in ASEAN-led mechanisms, particularly in discussions concerning maritime issues and the South China Sea. The ongoing efforts to finalise a COC in the South China Sea demonstrate both parties' commitment to peaceful dispute resolution and regional stability. China's participation in platforms such as the EAS and APT reinforces its influence in Southeast Asia, showcasing its dedication to security cooperation and economic integration.

Similarly, the ASEAN-Australia CSP, established in October 2021, builds upon nearly five decades of close cooperation. Being ASEAN's first Dialogue Partner since 1974, Australia has been essential in fostering strong bilateral ties that encompass strategic, economic, and socio-cultural dimensions. In 2022, two-way trade between ASEAN and Australia reached over $101 billion, bolstered by the AANZFTA. This agreement has facilitated the flow of goods, services, and investments across the region, reflecting the strong economic interconnections that have developed.

Australia's commitment to ASEAN's centrality in the Indo-Pacific is evident through its active participation in mechanisms such as the ARF, EAS and the ASEAN defence ADMM-Plus. The CSP emphasises maritime security, cybersecurity, and counter-terrorism cooperation, addressing shared concerns in an increasingly complex security environment. Furthermore, Australia has pledged support for ASEAN's climate resilience and infrastructure development by investing in green projects and sustainable development initiatives. Its development assistance to ASEAN exceeded $1 billion between 2018 and 2020, focusing on enhancing the region's disaster resilience, education, and health security.

The ASEAN-United States CSP, formalised in November 2022, signifies a new chapter in the enduring relationship between ASEAN and the United States. Since 1977, this relationship has grown to encompass various strategic and economic engagements. In 2022, two-way trade between ASEAN and the United States reached around $420 billion, reinforcing the United States as one of ASEAN's top trading partners. The CSP underscores the United States's commitment to promoting peace and stability in Southeast Asia, particularly through shared security interests like the vital issue of freedom of navigation in the South China Sea.

The United States actively engages in ASEAN-led mechanisms like the ARF, EAS and ADMM-Plus, contributing to discussions on regional security cooperation. Economically, the IPEF, launched in 2022, deepens United States economic ties with ASEAN. The IPEF targets vital areas, including digital trade, clean energy, and supply chain resilience, fostering sustainable economic growth and integration into global value chains. The United States stands as ASEAN's most significant FDI source, with cumulative investments surpassing $359.9 billion by 2022, further enhancing the region's technology, manufacturing, and services sectors.

The ASEAN-India CSP, established in 2022, reflects a relationship that has evolved significantly since India became an ASEAN Sectoral Dialogue Partner in 1992 and a Full Dialogue Partner in 1996. This partnership covers several areas, including strategic, economic, and socio-cultural cooperation. Two-way trade between ASEAN and India reached approximately $113 billion in 2022, supported by AIFTA, which came into force in 2010 and facilitates trade in goods, services, and investments. The CSP emphasises cooperation in maritime security, counterterrorism, and cybersecurity, with India remaining an active participant in ASEAN-led mechanisms, including the ARF, EAS and ADMM-Plus. India's Act East Policy has further strengthened ASEAN-India economic ties, focusing on enhancing infrastructure connectivity, digital trade, and supply chain resilience.

Cumulatively, India's FDI in ASEAN reached around $8 billion by 2022, making it a significant investor in sectors such as pharmaceuticals, technology, and services. Furthermore, India has provided development cooperation to ASEAN initiatives focused on education, public health, and capacity building through programs like the ASEAN-India Cooperation Fund, with investments exceeding $200 million since its establishment.

The elevation of ASEAN-Republic of Korea (ROK) relations to a Comprehensive Strategic Partnership (CSP) recently during the 25th ASEAN-ROK Summit in Vientiane, Laos, on 10 October 2024, marks a significant milestone in their cooperation since 1989. The CSP aims to strengthen collaboration in political-security, economic, and socio-cultural areas, enhancing peace, stability, and prosperity in the region.

Notably, in 2023, ASEAN-ROK trade reached USD 196.64 billion, despite an 11.7% decline from the previous year. The ROK maintained its position as ASEAN's fifth-largest trading partner. The ROK's foreign direct investment (FDI) in ASEAN amounted to USD 10.9 billion, making it the sixth-largest FDI source for ASEAN. This partnership reaffirms mutual commitments to international law, regional stability, and further integration through ASEAN-led mechanisms.

In short, ASEAN's role in international diplomacy has evolved significantly, and it has been characterised by the establishment of CSPs that enhance its influence on the world stage. The partnerships with key dialogue partners like China, the United States, Australia, and India underscore the interconnectedness of security, trade, and sustainable development within ASEAN's broader agenda. The establishment of future CSPs reflects ASEAN's continued commitment to enhancing its international engagement and strengthening ties with key external partners.

In this regard, New Zealand has indicated interest, which will likely be concluded at the ASEAN-New Zealand Commemorative Summit in 2025. As ASEAN addresses the complexities of international relations, it must balance its relationships with these major powers while maintaining its commitment to regional stability and cooperation.

ASEAN's role in multilateral diplomacy

ASEAN participates in major multilateral forums, including the United Nations (UN), the World Trade Organisation (WTO), and other international governance institutions. This role has been enhanced by ASEAN's consistent promotion of multilateralism, peaceful dispute resolution, and regional cooperation. It is a matter of pride to have strengthened itself diplomatically enough to be a robust voice in the international order. In this section, we will review some of ASEAN's multilateral partnerships.

ASEAN-UN cooperation

The Joint Declaration of the Comprehensive Partnership between ASEAN and the UN, established in 2011, has significantly strengthened ASEAN's engagement in global governance. This partnership covers several priority areas: peace and security, disaster risk reduction, sustainable development, and climate resilience. ASEAN has contributed to UN peacekeeping operations, deploying personnel and support in peace-building efforts across various global hotspots. ASEAN plays an active role in humanitarian relief efforts, providing timely assistance to disaster-affected regions within and beyond Southeast Asia. AHA Centre, in partnership with the UN Office for the Coordination of Humanitarian Affairs (OCHA), underscores ASEAN's commitment to global peace, security, and disaster response.

In the context of the UN's 2030 Agenda for Sustainable Development, ASEAN member states have aligned their national development plans with the SDGs, focusing on critical areas like poverty alleviation, education, and environmental sustainability. Initiatives such as the ASEAN Centre for Sustainable Development Studies and Dialogue (ACSDSD), established in 2019, are designed to facilitate research, dialogue, and collaboration on sustainable development goals within ASEAN and with global partners. The ASEAN Community Vision 2025 emphasises the integration of the SDGs into regional and national strategies, fostering partnerships with the UNDP, Environment Programme (UNEP), and other key UN agencies to achieve inclusive growth and sustainable development across Southeast Asia. ASEAN's cooperation with the UN also extends to climate action to enhance regional environmental policies, climate adaptation, and resilience strategies.

WTO and global trade diplomacy

ASEAN's engagement with the World Trade Organisation (WTO) has played a key role in integrating the region into the global trading system. ASEAN member states have advocated for fair trade practices, market access, and reducing NTBs through active participation in WTO negotiations. A notable achievement is the implementation of the WTO Trade Facilitation Agreement (TFA), which has significantly improved customs procedures across the region. Since its implementation in 2017, the TFA has led to an average reduction of about 5-6% in trade costs among ASEAN member states.

This improvement has enhanced intra-ASEAN trade and global trade flows, aligning with the region's broader economic integration and sustainable development goals. ASEAN's collective efforts in WTO negotiations have focused on critical areas such as agriculture, fisheries subsidies, and e-commerce, further supporting its trade facilitation and regional economic cooperation objectives.

Moreover, ASEAN member states have actively implemented customs reforms, digitisation initiatives, and capacity-building programs to streamline cross-border trade. The establishment of the ASW is a prime example of these efforts, enhancing trade connectivity and facilitating the efficient exchange of trade-related information. This collaborative framework boosts trade efficiency and fosters a more competitive environment for ASEAN economies on the global stage.

IMF and financial stability

ASEAN's partnership with the International Monetary Fund (IMF) is instrumental in ensuring the region's macroeconomic stability and financial resilience. The IMF Regional Office for Asia and the Pacific works closely with ASEAN member states to provide technical assistance in critical areas such as monetary policy, fiscal management, and financial sector development. This collaboration is vital for enhancing the region's capacity to manage economic challenges and maintain stability amid global uncertainties.

Key areas of cooperation between ASEAN and the IMF include economic policy coordination and capacity-building initiatives, which align with ASEAN's financial frameworks, such as the CMIM and the AMRO. The CMIM, established to provide liquidity support during financial crises, is complemented by AMRO's role in monitoring regional economies and providing timely economic assessments. Together, these initiatives aim to prevent and respond effectively to potential financial crises, ensuring that ASEAN member states are better equipped to handle economic shocks.

Furthermore, collaboration with the IMF has also facilitated the development of financial safety nets and improved regulatory frameworks across ASEAN. Member states are better positioned to enhance their financial systems and regulatory environments by engaging in capacity-building programs, fostering greater regional financial stability. This proactive approach bolsters individual economies and strengthens regional integration and resilience against external financial disruptions.

World Bank and development

ASEAN's collaboration with the World Bank Group is crucial for advancing sustainable development, poverty reduction, and regional infrastructure investment. The World Bank aligns its support closely with ASEAN's economic and social objectives, particularly by financing essential transportation, energy, and water supply projects. For example, the World Bank has supported enhancing regional connectivity by financing improved transport networks, which facilitate trade and mobility within ASEAN.

This is exemplified by the Southeast Asia Regional Economic Corridor and Connectivity Project, which aims to create climate-resilient transport connectivity to boost regional trade. Investments in energy projects focus on providing reliable and sustainable energy sources to underserved areas, essential for promoting equitable growth.

Moreover, the World Bank invests in human capital development by financing educational programs and healthcare initiatives that enhance the quality of life for ASEAN citizens. This focus on social welfare addresses inequalities and fosters inclusive development across member states. Besides, technical expertise from the World Bank supports initiatives like the ASW, which simplifies customs procedures to facilitate trade. The ASW is expected to enhance intra-ASEAN trade by streamlining documentation and reducing delays, thereby significantly reinforcing economic integration.

WHO and health security and preparedness

ASEAN's partnership with the WHO is pivotal in addressing public health challenges and enhancing health systems throughout Southeast Asia. This collaboration emphasises several key areas, including universal health coverage (UHC), disease surveillance, pandemic preparedness, and the management of non-communicable diseases (NCDs) and antimicrobial resistance (AMR). Together, ASEAN and the WHO work to foster a healthier, more resilient population by implementing evidence-based strategies and promoting health equity among member states.

One prominent example of this cooperation is the ASEAN COVID-19 Response Fund, established to bolster member states' pandemic management efforts. This fund has facilitated vaccine procurement and distribution, with the WHO providing critical technical guidance on implementing effective health measures. In addition, the ASEAN Post-2015 Health Development Agenda (APHDA) 2021-2025 addresses the rising threat of NCDs through regional campaigns that promote healthy lifestyles. The ASEAN Strategy on NCD Prevention and Control encourages member countries to adopt policies that mitigate risk factors such as tobacco use and poor nutrition.

Furthermore, with WHO's guidance and support, the Association has developed the ASEAN Framework for Action on AMR, which outlines strategies for improving surveillance, promoting responsible antimicrobial use, and raising public awareness about the risks associated with AMR. This comprehensive approach aims to tackle immediate health concerns and strengthen the overall resilience of health systems in the region, ultimately contributing to long-term health improvements across Southeast Asia.

Economic diplomacy and the Indo-Pacific strategy

ASEAN's economic diplomacy within the Indo-Pacific region is pivotal in managing the complex power dynamics among major global players, particularly China and the United States. By leveraging an extensive network of FTAs and economic partnerships, ASEAN enhances its strategic significance while promoting economic integration among its member states. This multifaceted approach bolsters ASEAN's economic resilience and amplifies its influence on regional stability, allowing the organisation to serve as a cohesive entity amidst shifting geopolitical landscapes.

The ASEAN Outlook on the Indo-Pacific (AOIP), adopted in 2019, is a foundational framework that underscores ASEAN's commitment to a rules-based order, inclusivity, and respect for sovereignty. The AOIP articulates a vision of a peaceful and stable Indo-Pacific region where economic cooperation, maritime security, and sustainable development are prioritised. This strategic vision positions ASEAN as a key player in shaping the future of the Indo-Pacific, fostering a regional environment that emphasises dialogue and cooperation rather than rivalry.

During the Laos ASEAN Summit in October 2024, ASEAN leaders reaffirmed their commitment to the AOIP, recognising its critical role in enhancing regional stability and cooperation. Plans were announced for the second

ASEAN-Indo-Pacific Forum, which will focus on regional sustainable development and connectivity initiatives. This forum aims to facilitate dialogue with key external powers, including Japan, the European Union, and the United States, reinforcing ASEAN's leadership and ensuring continued engagement with these critical partners.

Despite these advancements, the AOIP faces significant challenges, particularly due to geopolitical pressures and the proliferation of "minilateral" defence arrangements, such as the Australia-United Kingdom-United States trilateral security partnership (AUKUS) and the Quadrilateral Security Dialogue (Quad) comprising Australia, India, Japan, and the United States, which may undermine ASEAN's central role in the regional security architecture. Observers have pointed out that while the AOIP has been endorsed as a guiding framework, it requires a sharper focus on tangible outcomes to enhance its strategic relevance in the face of evolving dynamics.

ASEAN's engagement in initiatives like the RCEP further deepens regional economic ties and enhances its bargaining power with external partners. By reinforcing economic relationships through these strategic initiatives, ASEAN strengthens its internal cohesion and positions itself as a pivotal player on the global stage. Looking ahead, the implementation of the AOIP will continue to evolve, which is expected to prioritise connectivity and sustainable development, particularly through digital transformation and climate resilience initiatives. The commitment to operationalising the AOIP through concrete projects and activities reflects ASEAN's recognition of its growing significance in the Indo-Pacific and its potential to positively influence the regional economic landscape.

ASEAN's role in regional and global peace

In an increasingly volatile geopolitical environment, ASEAN has sought to maintain regional stability through regional security dialogues and active engagement with major powers on critical security issues. Through the ARF and EAS, ASEAN has facilitated multilateral discussions on key security challenges, including maritime disputes, terrorism, and nuclear proliferation.

The ARF is the Asia-Pacific's most comprehensive multilateral security forum. It brings together twenty-seven members, including ASEAN, its dialogue partners, and other players such as North Korea. The ARF focuses on confidence-building measures, preventive diplomacy, and conflict resolution and serves as a platform for dialogue on pressing security concerns. In recent years, the ARF has expanded its focus to address non-traditional security threats, such as cybercrime, climate change, and health pandemics. The ARF's role in promoting peace and stability in the region is especially important in the context of territorial disputes in the South China Sea. While these disputes have strained relations between ASEAN members and China, the ARF has provided a dialogue platform, reducing the escalation risk.

The EAS is another crucial platform for ASEAN's engagement in regional security. Established in 2005, the EAS brings together ASEAN members and key major powers, including the United States, China, Russia, and India, to discuss strategic and security issues in the broader Asia-Pacific region. The EAS has been pivotal in addressing maritime security, nuclear proliferation, and transnational crime challenges. The EAS's discussions on the South China Sea, the North Korean nuclear issue, and regional counterterrorism efforts have underscored ASEAN's centrality in facilitating regional security dialogues. The EAS has also expanded its focus to include climate security, recognising the growing impact of climate change on regional peace and stability.

ASEAN's security cooperation with external partners has been vital in addressing terrorism, human trafficking, and other forms of transnational crime. The ASEAN Convention on Counter-Terrorism (ACCT) and the establishment of regional initiatives like the ASEAN Plan of Action to Combat Transnational Crime have strengthened ASEAN's ability to confront these challenges. ASEAN's collaboration with international partners, particularly the United States, Australia, and Japan, has enhanced its capacity to respond to the growing threat of ISIS-inspired extremist groups in Southeast Asia. Regional cooperation on intelligence sharing, capacity building, and border security has played a vital role in preventing attacks and dismantling terrorist networks.

ASEAN's contribution to climate action and sustainable development

ASEAN, one of the world's most climate-vulnerable regions, has assumed a proactive leadership role in advocating climate action and sustainable development on a global scale. Therefore, ASEAN's contribution to climate change diplomacy is of due importance. Member states have prioritised decreasing greenhouse gas emissions, boosting the use of renewable energy, and improving climate resilience through national strategies. For example, the APAEC 2016-2025 lays out ambitious goals for expanding renewable energy's contribution to the region's energy mix to 23% by 2025. Furthermore, initiatives such as the ASEAN Action Plan on Joint Response to Climate Change (AAP-JRCC) aim to strengthen regional cooperation in climate mitigation and adaptation by providing a systematic framework for member nations to coordinate their responses.

At the regional level, the ASEAN Working Group on Climate Change (AWGCC) facilitates cooperation among member states. The AWGCC prioritises several critical topics, including promoting renewable energy technology, improving catastrophe risk reduction methods, and implementing sustainable land use practices. The ASEAN Disaster Emergency Response

Simulation Exercise (DERS) is an example of successful regional collaboration that strengthens ASEAN nations' ability to respond effectively to natural catastrophes aggravated by climate change. ASEAN's dedication to sustainable development is inextricably connected to the UN SDGs. The region has had significant success in various sectors, including poverty alleviation, education, health care, and environmental protection. ASEAN member states show their collective commitment to achieving these global goals by incorporating the SDGs into their national development plans. The ACSDSD encourages the exchange of best practices for sustainable development and collaboration with international agencies such as the World Bank and ADB.

For example, partnership with the ADB has resulted in programs to increase urban resilience in ASEAN cities and mitigate climate risks while supporting sustainable infrastructure. Projects like the Sustainable Transport Infrastructure Development Project strive to improve urban transportation networks by using climate adaptation techniques to strengthen their resilience to climate impacts. Furthermore, ASEAN's participation in international forums such as the United Nations Framework Convention on Climate Change (UNFCCC) and COP meetings demonstrates its determination to participate actively in global climate governance. ASEAN uses various forums to advocate for its member states' interests while also establishing a common voice on topics such as climate funding, technology transfer, and capacity building.

Challenges to ASEAN's global engagement

While ASEAN has strengthened its global engagement and regional integration over the decades, it faces multiple challenges that test its centrality, effectiveness, and ability to maintain its role as a key actor on the world stage.

ASEAN's ability to balance relationships with major powers, particularly the United States and China, has become increasingly complex in recent years. The South China Sea dispute remains a significant flashpoint in ASEAN-China relations, with overlapping territorial claims by ASEAN member states and China creating regional tensions. Although ASEAN has continued to engage China diplomatically through mechanisms like the ARF and ongoing negotiations for a COC, progress remains slow, and member states must navigate China's growing assertiveness in the region. Simultaneously, the United States has increased its strategic focus on the Indo-Pacific, promoting freedom of navigation and the IPEF to enhance economic ties. This shift has pressured ASEAN to align with broader geopolitical interests and reinforce its strategic autonomy. Balancing these competing influences without compromising its unity and centrality becomes critical for ASEAN's ability to maintain relevance in regional diplomacy and as a bridge between major powers.

Global trade shifts and supply chain disruptions, mainly resulting from the United States-China trade war, the COVID-19 pandemic, and geopolitical shifts, have posed significant challenges for ASEAN economies. The trade war has led to some supply chain diversification, with countries like Vietnam and Thailand benefiting from the relocation of manufacturing and investment flows. However, ASEAN faces uncertainties in global trade, and intra-ASEAN trade accounted for only 22% of the region's total trade in 2022, indicating a need for further integration and trade facilitation.

ASEAN has prioritised trade liberalisation through regional agreements such as the RCEP, which is expected to add $245 billion annually to the global economy by 2030 to enhance economic resilience and mitigate risks posed by external trade conflicts. ASEAN's emphasis on digital economy initiatives, e-commerce, and regional connectivity also aims to position the region to capitalise on new trade opportunities and supply chain resilience.

Southeast Asia is highly vulnerable to climate change's impacts, including extreme weather events, rising sea levels, deforestation, and transboundary environmental issues like air pollution and haze. According to the ADB, these environmental challenges have significant economic and social consequences, with climate change projected to reduce ASEAN's GDP by up to 11% by 2100. ASEAN has strengthened regional cooperation on environmental sustainability and disaster resilience to tackle this situation through frameworks like the AATHP, the ASEAN Climate Change Initiative, and APAEC.

While progress has been made, significant challenges remain in securing international support for climate mitigation and adaptation efforts. The ASEAN Centre for Climate Change and partnerships with global actors like the UNDP and Green Climate Fund (GCF) aim to build capacity, mobilise financing, and promote green growth in the region. However, ASEAN must enhance policy coordination, resource mobilisation, and capacity-building to implement its environmental and climate objectives fully.

ASEAN's growing influence in global diplomacy, trade, and security has solidified its role as an emerging player in international affairs. Through its extensive network of dialogue partners and active participation in multilateral institutions such as the United Nations, World Trade Organisation (WTO), and ASEAN-led forums, ASEAN has effectively navigated an intricate global landscape while maintaining its centrality in the regional architecture. Trade agreements like the RCEP and ASEAN FTAs and cooperation with major powers like China, the United States, Japan, and the European Union have bolstered ASEAN's economic integration and enhanced its voice in regional security and global governance.

Looking ahead, ASEAN must address emerging challenges such as great power competition, particularly between the United States and China, global trade disruptions driven by supply chain shifts and economic uncertainties, and the growing impacts of climate change on the region's economy, environment, and livelihoods. Enhancing internal cohesion, promoting intra-ASEAN trade, and fortifying institutional mechanisms to respond to external pressures will be crucial to ASEAN's continued success. By leveraging its existing regional frameworks and deepening its collaboration on non-traditional security issues like public health, environmental sustainability, and digital economy, ASEAN can better respond to the changing global dynamics.

ASEAN will need to balance relations with major powers, mitigate economic vulnerabilities, and enhance climate resilience through sustainable practices and green technologies. By strengthening its global partnerships, fostering multilateralism, and reinforcing its commitment to a rules-based regional order, ASEAN can continue to be a vital force in contributing to global governance and ensuring peace, stability, and prosperity in the Asia-Pacific region.

> *"ASEAN's global engagement reflects its growing influence as a key actor in regional and international affairs. ASEAN ensures that Southeast Asia remains an integral part of the global order by building strategic partnerships and enhancing its role in global governance. The future of ASEAN lies in its ability to*

balance regional priorities with global responsibilities, shaping a more interconnected and resilient world."

Pushpanathan Sundram, Author

Chapter 12

ASEAN Centrality – Maintaining Relevance in a Multipolar World

"We further reaffirmed our commitment to strengthening the ASEAN Community, its unity and Centrality. We reiterated the importance of maintaining an ASEAN-centred, open, inclusive, transparent, resilient, and rules-based regional architecture that upholds international law and of strengthening our engagement and cooperation with Dialogue Partners and external partners, including through existing ASEAN-led mechanisms, in promoting peace, stability, security, development, and growth to enhance our regional resilience to respond to common and emerging challenges."

Joint Communique of the 57th ASEAN Foreign Ministers' Meeting, Vientiane, July 25, 2024

The principle of ASEAN centrality is fundamental to the organisation's identity and vital for its role in regional governance. This concept emphasises ASEAN's aspiration to be the primary platform for cooperation on political, security, and economic matters among its member states and with external partners in Southeast Asia. In a world increasingly characterised by multipolarity, where various nations assert their influence, ASEAN's ability to maintain its centrality is essential for ensuring peace and stability in the region. ASEAN centrality promotes an inclusive approach to regional governance, facilitating collective action among member states to address pressing challenges while engaging constructively with external powers. This principle is embodied in ASEAN-led initiatives that emphasise multilateralism and cooperative security. However, ASEAN faces significant challenges, particularly from the escalating contestation between the United States and China, the emergence of alternative regional frameworks, and internal divisions among member states. This chapter will explore the historical evolution of ASEAN centrality, the principles underpinning it, the contemporary challenges it faces, and the strategies ASEAN employs to reinforce its relevance amid shifting geopolitical dynamics.

Evolution of ASEAN centrality

ASEAN was founded in 1967 in a geopolitical context marked by Cold War tensions. The founding members recognised the urgent need to foster peace and stability through regional cooperation. They articulated a commitment to non-interference and consensus-based decision-making, which became central to ASEAN's diplomatic approach. The historical context of ASEAN's establishment underscores its central philosophy. Managing regional conflicts and external pressures necessitated a diplomatic culture prioritising dialogue and mutual respect. This approach facilitated cooperation among diverse political systems and positioned ASEAN as a stabilising force in Southeast Asia. The early emphasis on economic cooperation paved the way for deeper political integration, fostering a sense of collective identity and dependence among member states.

The establishment of the ARF in 1994 marked a pivotal moment in ASEAN's commitment to centrality. The ARF became the first multilateral security dialogue platform in Asia, allowing ASEAN to engage key external powers—including the United States, China, Japan, Russia, and India—and facilitate discussions on critical security issues. The ARF's emphasis on preventive diplomacy and confidence-building measures reinforced ASEAN's position as an interlocuter in regional conflicts. This proactive approach enhanced regional stability and allowed ASEAN to address complex security challenges collaboratively. ASEAN established itself as a critical player in shaping the regional security architecture by facilitating discussions among diverse stakeholders.

ASEAN's role in the ARF exemplifies its strategy of fostering dialogue to prevent conflict, reflecting its historical commitment to maintaining regional peace. As a result, ASEAN has been able to steer the intricate relationships among its member states and external powers, promoting an environment conducive to cooperation and mutual understanding.

Navigating geopolitical complexity

Despite its historical achievements, ASEAN now faces various challenges that threaten its centrality in regional and global affairs. The rise of major powers, particularly the United States and China, and the emergence of alternative multilateral frameworks necessitate that ASEAN navigate an increasingly intricate geopolitical landscape. This dynamic is especially pronounced as both superpowers vie for influence in the Indo-Pacific region, placing ASEAN in a precarious position where it must balance its relationships without compromising its neutral stance.

The intensifying contestation between the United States and China profoundly impacts ASEAN's role as a key mediator. The South China Sea dispute is a significant flashpoint, with overlapping territorial claims among ASEAN member states and China heightening regional tensions. While ASEAN has continued diplomatic engagement with China through mechanisms like the ARF and ongoing negotiations for a COC, progress has been slow. Member states are increasingly aware of the need to carefully steer China's growing assertiveness.

China's Belt and Road initiative (BRI) has further complicated this balance, significantly expanding China's economic influence in Southeast Asia. While some ASEAN member states welcome Chinese investments for their potential to boost development and infrastructure, others harbour concerns about dependency and sovereignty. The fear is that heavy reliance on Chinese funding could jeopardise national autonomy, prompting a dual perspective within ASEAN. This complexity highlights the delicate task of balancing economic benefits with foreign investment risks.

In response, the United States has increased its regional strategic presence through initiatives like the IPEF and various military partnerships to counter China's influence. This United States pivot forces ASEAN to navigate external pressures while reinforcing its identity as a neutral mediator. The establishment of the AUKUS alliance—comprising Australia, the United Kingdom, and the United States—further exemplifies the challenges ASEAN faces in maintaining its centrality. Diverging views on AUKUS among member states, with some supporting enhanced security cooperation and others expressing concerns about potential military tensions, underline the difficulties ASEAN encounters in forming a unified stance on security issues amidst external pressures.

The rise of alternative multilateral frameworks, such as the CPTPP and BRICS, adds another layer of complexity to ASEAN's role. While some ASEAN members actively participate in these frameworks, others remain excluded, raising questions about ASEAN's ability to act as a cohesive force in regional economic governance. These alternative partnerships present opportunities for enhanced economic cooperation but also risk overshadowing ASEAN's traditional role as the primary platform for trade and investment policies.

ASEAN's internal cohesion is vital for maintaining its centrality, but diverging national interests and political priorities often complicate collective decision-making. The South China Sea dispute exemplifies this internal discord, with countries like Vietnam and the Philippines advocating for a firmer stance against China. In contrast, others, such as Cambodia and Laos, prefer closer ties with Beijing. This lack of consensus threatens to weaken ASEAN's negotiating power and its ability to present a unified front in regional forums.

Historically, the ASEAN Way, characterised by consensus-based decision-making, has fostered unity among member states. However, it can impede timely responses to pressing challenges in a rapidly changing geopolitical environment. To adapt, ASEAN must strengthen its internal mechanisms for coordination and decision-making, particularly concerning non-traditional security issues like climate change, public health, and digital economy initiatives.

Looking ahead, ASEAN's ability to maintain relevance hinges on its capacity to balance relations with major powers, mitigate economic vulnerabilities, and enhance climate resilience through sustainable practices and green technologies. By reinforcing its commitment to a rules-based regional order and strengthening global partnerships, ASEAN can continue to play a vital role in shaping the future of global governance while ensuring peace, stability, and prosperity in the Asia-Pacific region.

ASEAN's strategies to maintain centrality

In the face of a rapidly evolving geopolitical landscape, ASEAN proactively implements strategies to bolster its centrality in regional and global governance. Recognising the multifaceted challenges posed by major power rivalries, emerging multilateral frameworks, and the need for internal cohesion, ASEAN focuses on enhancing its institutional frameworks, engaging effectively with dialogue partners, and promoting comprehensive initiatives.

A cornerstone of ASEAN's strategy involves strengthening its regional institutions such as the ARF, APT, EAS, and ADMM-Plus. These frameworks are crucial for addressing emerging security and economic challenges while engaging external partners. For instance, expanding the ARF's agenda to include pressing issues like cybersecurity, health security, and climate change will ensure ASEAN remains relevant in contemporary discussions. Furthermore, the EAS can enhance its focus on sustainable development and regional connectivity, reinforcing ASEAN's leadership in shaping global and regional dialogues.

Engaging effectively with dialogue partners is also essential for maintaining ASEAN's centrality. The organisation actively promotes inclusive multilateralism, ensuring that all major players are involved in regional dialogues under ASEAN's leadership. Convening ASEAN+1 summits facilitates the development of robust bilateral relationships while allowing ASEAN to retain its pivotal role in broader regional discussions. Frameworks like ASEAN+3 and the EAS exemplify ASEAN's capacity to unite external powers and reinforce its central role in diplomacy and cooperation.

The ASEAN Outlook on the Indo-Pacific (AOIP), adopted in 2019, positions ASEAN at the forefront of discussions on economic cooperation, maritime security, and regional stability in the Indo-Pacific. The AOIP emphasises ASEAN's commitment to inclusivity, openness, and respect for international law, which are essential for fostering collaborative relationships among member states and external partners. ASEAN promotes its vision for a rules-based order through its proactive engagement in Indo-Pacific dialogues, enabling stakeholders to collaborate on shared interests such as trade, climate change, and disaster management.

Moreover, ASEAN's emphasis on regional connectivity through initiatives like the MPAC 2025 further enhances its centrality by promoting sustainable infrastructure development, digital integration, and people-to-people connectivity. This comprehensive approach strengthens ASEAN's role in the Indo-Pacific and increases its capacity to address common challenges collaboratively.

By leveraging these strategies, ASEAN seeks to navigate the complexities of the current geopolitical environment, reinforcing its relevance as a key player in shaping regional stability and fostering prosperity in the Indo-Pacific. The organisation must continue to adapt and evolve to maintain its central position amidst the dynamic interactions of global powers.

ASEAN centrality in global governance

ASEAN's influence extends well beyond its regional borders, positioning itself as a constructive player in global governance through its active participation in international organisations, trade agreements, and climate initiatives. As a collective voice for Southeast Asia, ASEAN's global engagement strengthens its role as a regional leader and enhances its capacity to address pressing international challenges.

ASEAN's leadership in global economic governance is notably exemplified by its involvement in the RCEP. This monumental agreement includes ASEAN member states and key dialogue partners, representing approximately 30% of the world's GDP. The successful negotiation and implementation of RCEP underscore ASEAN's ability to drive international trade dynamics while asserting its centrality in regional economic integration. By creating a comprehensive trade framework, RCEP facilitates trade liberalisation and economic cooperation, demonstrating

ASEAN's commitment to fostering a robust economic environment in the Asia-Pacific.

Furthermore, ASEAN's active participation in global forums, such as the G20 and the World Trade Organisation (WTO), provides it with platforms to advocate for the interests of its member states. Through these engagements, ASEAN emphasises the importance of cooperation and mutual benefit in discussions about international trade policies and economic recovery strategies, particularly in the aftermath of the COVID-19 pandemic. This active participation in global governance reinforces ASEAN's relevance and positions it as a vital player in shaping responses to international economic challenges.

Besides economic governance, ASEAN is deeply involved in global climate governance, especially given its vulnerability to climate change impacts. All member states are signatories to the Paris Agreement, committing to their Nationally Determined Contributions (NDCs) to reduce greenhouse gas emissions and enhance climate resilience. ASEAN's collaboration in initiatives such as the AATHP exemplifies its commitment to addressing environmental issues collectively. This agreement reflects ASEAN's determination to combat transboundary haze and showcases its role in fostering regional cooperation on environmental sustainability.

In 2021, ASEAN launched the ASEAN Green Bond Standards to promote sustainable financing for infrastructure projects, highlighting its commitment to sustainable development. By integrating environmental considerations into its economic policies, ASEAN addresses the immediate challenges of climate change while strengthening its position as a leader in global sustainable development efforts. This initiative reflects a growing recognition that economic growth and environmental sustainability must go hand in hand, paving the way for a more resilient and sustainable future for the region.

Through these comprehensive strategies, ASEAN enhances its centrality in global governance and demonstrates its commitment to fostering a cooperative and sustainable international environment. This multifaceted approach allows ASEAN to navigate the complexities of global dynamics while maintaining its relevance as a crucial player in addressing pressing global issues.

The future of ASEAN centrality: prospects and challenges

As ASEAN enters a new era, the future of its centrality in global governance is becoming increasingly significant amid an evolving geopolitical landscape. The organisation faces numerous challenges that test its adaptability and resilience, particularly in a world marked by multipolarity and intense great power rivalry. Yet, these challenges also present opportunities for ASEAN to redefine its role and strengthen its influence in the region and beyond.

For example, a prominent concern is the strategic competition between the United States and China, which has become a defining feature of the geopolitical environment. Both nations are vital economic partners for ASEAN member states; however, their conflicting interests complicate regional dynamics. To navigate this complex rivalry, ASEAN must adopt a strategy of strategic hedging, allowing member states to engage with both powers while Maintaining regional stability requires cultivating a united front among its members and fostering a collaborative approach to ensure that the interests of all countries are effectively represented in discussions with external powers. The challenge is to mitigate the risks of polarisation while maximising the potential benefits of engagement with both the United States and China.

The internal cohesion of its member states is central to ASEAN's ability to project its influence. Divergent national interests can complicate consensus-building, particularly on sensitive issues such as the South China Sea disputes and economic cooperation. This lack of consensus can weaken ASEAN's negotiating power and diminish its effectiveness as a regional body. ASEAN must prioritise the development of a shared regional identity to foster unity. Initiatives that promote cultural exchange, educational cooperation, and tourism can enhance mutual understanding among member states, ultimately leading to a more cohesive ASEAN community. A strong sense of ASEAN identity will improve collective bargaining power and ensure that all member states' interests are effectively represented in regional dialogues.

Strengthening the ASEAN Secretariat and enhancing its institutional mechanisms are crucial for effectively addressing the complex challenges of an increasingly multipolar world. The Secretariat serves as the core administrative body that coordinates activities, facilitates cooperation among member states, and implements ASEAN initiatives. Further reforms will be necessary to optimise its impact and relevance. One essential step towards enhancing the Secretariat's effectiveness is investing in capacity building and professionalisation, including the local staff. A well-trained human resource capacity equipped with strategic planning, negotiation, and policy analysis skills will enable the Secretariat to support member states better. Current discussions emphasise the need to attract qualified professionals to the Secretariat by improving funding and resources, creating a virtuous cycle of talent acquisition and retention.

Establishing specialised task forces within the Secretariat can facilitate targeted responses to pressing issues such as cybersecurity, public health emergencies, and disaster management. Given Southeast Asia's vulnerability to natural disasters, enhancing disaster preparedness and response mechanisms through these task forces can significantly improve ASEAN's effectiveness. Such specialised groups can draw on expertise from member states and partner organisations, allowing for a more agile and coordinated approach to addressing critical challenges.

Moreover, think tanks such as the ASEAN Institutes of Strategic and International Studies (ASEAN-ISIS) and the Economic Research Institute of ASEAN and East Asia (ERIA) are integral to strengthening ASEAN's institutional capacity and should provide more opportunities to collaborate with the ASEAN Secretariat. ASEAN-ISIS could be supportive in providing strategic insights and fostering dialogue on critical issues impacting the region, acting as a bridge between policymakers and academia. Its work ensures that evidence-based recommendations are integrated into ASEAN's initiatives, particularly in shaping regional security and economic cooperation discussions. Similarly, the ERIA focuses on economic research and policy recommendations supporting ASEAN's economic integration and development goals, conducting comprehensive analyses of trade and investment issues vital for navigating economic challenges in a globalised economy.

These are active avenues for solution-oriented thinking; for instance, the inaugural ASEAN Think Tanks Summit (ATTS) in Jakarta in September 2024 was organised by the ASEAN-ISIS in collaboration with the ASEAN Secretariat to improve regional cooperation and address geopolitical and economic issues. Thought leaders and representatives from think tanks and dialogue partners attended the summit to discuss important matters ahead of ASEAN

Summits. The discussions identified five key areas: digital connectivity, energy connectivity, institutional and political connectivity, ASEAN centrality, and AOIP operationalisation. The summit stressed collaborative policymaking and is expected to lead to continued conversations to strengthen ASEAN's ability to address conventional and non-traditional security threats.

ASEAN can create a more robust intellectual foundation for its initiatives by fostering deeper partnerships with think tanks and civil society. Joint research projects, targeted training programs, and dialogue forums can facilitate the integration of expert insights into ASEAN's policy-making processes, enhancing its credibility and effectiveness in addressing regional challenges. Ultimately, the future of ASEAN's centrality hinges on its ability to adapt and innovate in response to the dynamic geopolitical landscape. By embracing inclusivity and collaboration, ASEAN can reaffirm its role as a central force in regional stability and prosperity. As the organisation navigates the complexities of a multipolar world, maintaining an ASEAN-centred approach will enhance its relevance and ensure that it remains a vital contributor to global governance and a beacon of hope for its member states.

> *"ASEAN centrality is the foundation of its success in navigating a multipolar world. By maintaining its role as the convener of regional dialogue and cooperation, ASEAN ensures that it remains relevant and*

influential amidst shifting global power dynamics. Its ability to bring diverse powers to the table underscores its importance in maintaining regional stability and coherence in an increasingly complex world."

Pushpanathan Sundram, Author

Chapter 13

Ten Lessons from ASEAN: Fifty Years of Regional Cooperation & Growth

"We have every reason to be optimistic about our future and the future of ASEAN. The ingredients we need are scalability, replicability, and willpower. But to hold it together, we need one another. We need unity, we need cooperation."

World Bank President Ajay Banga at the ASEAN Summit, 5 September 2023, Jakarta, Indonesia

As we look back on over fifty years of ASEAN's existence, it is clear that the Association has played an indispensable role in shaping Southeast Asia into a region of stability, growth, and increasing global relevance. From its modest beginnings in 1967 as a platform for peace and dialogue among the five founding nations, ASEAN has transformed into a dynamic, multifaceted organisation that addresses everything from economic integration to environmental sustainability.

The journey has been far from easy. ASEAN has navigated many challenges: Cold War-era conflicts, economic crises, territorial disputes, and, most recently, the global COVID-19 pandemic. Despite these hurdles, the organisation has emerged stronger, adapting and evolving while staying true to its core principles of cooperation, consensus, and respect for sovereignty.

This chapter discusses ten critical lessons from ASEAN's half-century of experience in regional diplomacy and integration. These insights highlight what has made ASEAN successful and provide a roadmap for how the Association can thrive in an increasingly complex world. We can appreciate ASEAN's unique role in the Asia-Pacific region and beyond by understanding these foundational lessons.

These lessons speak to ASEAN's resilience, adaptability, and commitment to regional harmony. From the power of consensus to the ability to navigate geopolitical tensions, ASEAN's cooperation model offers valuable insights for anyone interested in international relations and regional governance. These key learnings also reflect how regional organisations can effectively face global challenges.

1. Consensus as a pillar of unity

ASEAN's consensus-based decision-making process has been integral to maintaining its unity. Unlike organisations that make decisions through majority voting, ASEAN's approach ensures that all members have an equal say regardless of size or power. This method has been vital in keeping countries with diverse political systems—from democracies like Indonesia to monarchies like Brunei—on the same page. While this can lead to slower decision-making, it prevents domination by any one country and fosters an atmosphere of cooperation. The spirit of consensus, enshrined in the 1976 TAC, continues to be a cornerstone of ASEAN's resilience.

2. Non-interference: a vital principle, but not without its challenges

ASEAN's principle of non-interference, formalised in the TAC in 1976 and the ASEAN Charter of 2007, has allowed the region to respect the sovereignty of each member state, preventing external meddling in domestic issues. This has been essential in maintaining trust between states with different internal challenges, such as political unrest or economic instability. However, the non-interference policy has also been tested, especially during the Rohingya crisis and Myanmar's military coup in 2021. ASEAN's response, including the Five-Point Consensus on Myanmar, highlights this principle's strengths and limitations. Balancing non-interference with regional stability will remain an ongoing challenge.

3. Adaptability: ASEAN's greatest strength

ASEAN has proven to be highly adaptable over its five decades of existence. Starting as a regional organisation focused primarily on political stability, ASEAN has successfully expanded its mandate to include economic integration, environmental sustainability, and social cooperation. The AEC formation in 2015 marked a significant milestone in economic integration, creating a single market and production base. ASEAN has also responded to emerging issues such as climate change, cyber security, and public health, including its coordinated efforts during the COVID-19 pandemic. This adaptability has allowed ASEAN to remain relevant in a rapidly changing global environment, ensuring its members can respond effectively to regional and global challenges.

4. ASEAN centrality: leading regional diplomacy

ASEAN has carved out a vital role for itself in the broader Asia-Pacific region through what is known as ASEAN centrality. This concept means that ASEAN serves as the hub for dialogue and cooperation among major powers in the region, ensuring that Southeast Asia remains a neutral zone amid rising geopolitical tensions. Through initiatives like the ARF and the EAS, ASEAN has positioned itself to become a key player in diplomatic discussions, engaging major powers like China, the United States, Japan, and India. Maintaining this role will be critical as the Indo-Pacific region becomes increasingly contested by the United States and China.

5. Open regionalism: a gateway to the world

ASEAN's commitment to open regionalism has allowed it to maintain strong connections with external partners without compromising its autonomy. ASEAN has secured its place in global trade and diplomacy by fostering dialogue and cooperation through its 11 dialogue partners, which include major powers like the United States, China, and the European Union. The success of agreements like the ASEAN Free Trade Area (AFTA) and RCEP exemplifies ASEAN's ability to engage in global trade while maintaining its regional identity.

Open regionalism has ensured ASEAN remains an attractive partner for regional and global powers, striking a balance between fostering external relations and protecting its core regional interests. This approach strengthened ASEAN's influence and gave its member states greater leverage in international trade negotiations. By positioning itself as a hub for trade and diplomacy, ASEAN has enhanced its role in shaping regional norms and setting an example for other regional organisations worldwide.

6. Economic integration: a driving force of prosperity

The launch of the AEC in 2015 was a landmark achievement, marking ASEAN's most ambitious attempt to integrate the economies of its member states into a single market and production base. The AEC has lowered trade barriers, enhanced regional connectivity, and attracted foreign investment, contributing to the region's economic dynamism. While progress has been uneven, with disparities between member states like Singapore and Laos, the AEC has nevertheless created a more integrated market, fostering greater economic cooperation and resilience. ASEAN's strong performance in global value chains, particularly in manufacturing and services, highlights the tangible benefits of economic integration.

7. Social and cultural cooperation: building a sense of community

Beyond economics and diplomacy, ASEAN has increasingly emphasised social and cultural cooperation. Through initiatives like the ASCC, ASEAN has sought to promote greater people-to-people connections across Southeast Asia. Programs like student exchange scholarships, youth forums, and cultural festivals have helped foster a shared ASEAN identity, especially among the younger generations. The increased awareness of ASEAN among its citizens, particularly in education, health, and disaster management, has strengthened the region's sense of community. However, building a more inclusive and equitable ASEAN remains a work in progress, with efforts underway to address social inequalities across member states.

8. Sustainable development and environmental responsibility

ASEAN's commitment to sustainable development has grown in response to the region's vulnerability to climate change and environmental degradation. The region has taken steps to address pressing environmental issues, including air pollution, deforestation, and rising sea levels, through initiatives like the AATHP and the ASEAN Climate Change Initiative. Given the region's susceptibility to natural disasters like typhoons, floods, and earthquakes, ASEAN's efforts in disaster risk reduction and climate adaptation have been particularly significant. Although challenges remain, particularly in balancing economic growth with environmental protection, ASEAN's focus on sustainability is critical to its long-term vision for the region.

9. Navigating geopolitical rivalries

As tensions rise between major powers, especially the United States and China, ASEAN has played a delicate balancing act in navigating these rivalries. The South

China Sea, a key geopolitical flashpoint, has tested ASEAN's diplomatic abilities. While ASEAN has not always been able to present a unified front on the issue, it has managed to engage China in discussions on the Code of Conduct for the South China Sea, which aims to reduce regional tensions. ASEAN's strength lies in its ability to maintain neutrality and avoid being drawn into the orbit of any one power. Through mechanisms like the ASEAN-China Free Trade Agreement and participation in broader regional groupings such as the EAS, ASEAN continues engaging with China and the United States while preserving its autonomy.

10. Resilience through crisis: lessons from economic and health shocks

ASEAN has shown remarkable resilience in responding to crises, particularly during the Asian Financial Crisis of 1997 and the recent COVID-19 pandemic. The Asian Financial Crisis was a turning point for ASEAN, prompting member states to implement structural reforms and enhance economic cooperation. This laid the groundwork for forming the Chiang Mai Initiative (CMI), a multilateral currency swap arrangement that has become the region's key financial safety net. The CMIM initiative highlights ASEAN's commitment to regional financial stability and cooperation.

Similarly, ASEAN's response to the COVID-19 pandemic demonstrated its ability to coordinate public health measures and economic recovery efforts across its member states. The establishment of the COVID-19 ASEAN Response Fund and the ASEAN Comprehensive Recovery Framework (ACRF) showed how quickly the region could mobilise resources to address public health crises while also mitigating economic fallout. These experiences underscore ASEAN's resilience and ability to adapt and recover from economic shocks and health emergencies.

Through these key characteristics, ASEAN has proven itself to be a model of regional cooperation, balancing the interests of its member states with the need for broader regional and global engagement. From consensus decision-making to its non-interference principle, ASEAN has created a unique framework that continues to evolve in the face of global challenges. As ASEAN moves forward, its ability to adapt, promote inclusivity, and maintain a role in regional diplomacy will determine its future success. By learning from the past and embracing future challenges, ASEAN will remain a vital player in the regional and global order.

> *"The key lessons from ASEAN's 50 years of regional cooperation and growth lie in its commitment to consensus, respect for sovereignty, and inclusivity. ASEAN's ability to adapt to changing geopolitical landscapes while maintaining unity is a testament to its resilience. These lessons provide valuable insights*

for the region and governance in an increasingly interconnected world."

Pushpanathan Sundram, Author

Bonus Chapter 14

50 Fascinating Facts about ASEAN in Numbers

> *ASEAN has great economic growth potential. ASEAN economic growth in 2024 is estimated to be the highest in the world, reaching 4.5 percent (year on year)........ ASEAN is the most attractive region for foreign direct investment. In, 2022, 17 percent of the global foreign direct investment will be in ASEAN, the highest number compared to other developing regions.......ASEAN also has a demographic bonus with the third largest workforce in the world, while as much as 65 percent of the population in ASEAN has the potential to become middle class by 2030.*
>
> ***President Jokowi Widodo of Indonesia, at the 2023 ASEAN Business Investment Summit at the State Palace, Jakarta, Indonesia, September 1, 2023***

Welcome to this exciting bonus chapter, which examines ASEAN's incredible path through compelling statistics. In this section, I present fifty remarkable facts that depict the commendable list of ASEAN's accomplishments and problems. These numbers are more than just data; they convey a fascinating tale about people's lives in this diverse region. As you analyse these facts, you will learn how ASEAN has become the world's fifth-largest economy, the importance of its young population in fuelling innovation, and the extraordinary progress made in intra- and extra-regional commerce. Each fact exemplifies ASEAN's dedication to cooperation, economic integration, and social progress, vividly depicting a region poised for expansion in an increasingly complicated global scene.

Prepare to be engaged as I offer fifty interesting facts over ten categories, each demonstrating ASEAN's resiliency and collaborative attitude. Exploring the figures will help you understand how ASEAN continues to shape its future and its critical role on the global stage.

Population and demographics

1. **680 million people:** As of 2023, ASEAN's population was approximately 680 million, making it the third-largest population globally after China and India.

2. **10 member states:** ASEAN consists of 10 member states: Brunei Darussalam, Cambodia, Indonesia, Lao PDR, Malaysia, Myanmar, the Philippines, Singapore, Thailand, and Vietnam.

3. **8.3% of the global population**: ASEAN is one of the most populous regions in the world, making up 8.3%, and

it has a significant demographic advantage, particularly in its young and growing workforce.

4. **50% youthful population:** Over 50% of ASEAN's population is under 30, providing a significant demographic advantage for economic growth and innovation.

5. **700 million people by 2030**: ASEAN's population is projected to surpass 700 million by 2030, driven by steady growth in countries like Indonesia and the Philippines.

6. **55% urbanisation population by 2030**: More than 55% of ASEAN's population will live in urban areas by 2030.

ASEAN as an economic power

7. **5th largest economy:** ASEAN's combined GDP exceeded $3.6 trillion in 2022, making it the fifth-largest economy globally.

8. **22% intra-ASEAN trade:** Intra-ASEAN trade accounts for 22% of ASEAN's total trade, valued at over $830.4 billion in 2022. For 2023, the preliminary figure is $900.7 billion or 22.5% of the region's total trade.

9. **99% of tariffs eliminated:** Under the ASEAN Free Trade Area (AFTA), 99% of tariffs on goods traded within ASEAN have been eliminated, promoting freer trade.

10. **$225 billion in FDI**: In 2022, ASEAN attracted $225 billion in foreign direct investment (FDI) inflows, a 23% increase compared to the previous year, positioning it as a critical global investment hub.

11. **$5,395 GDP per capita:** Most ASEAN countries will have achieved middle-income status, with the region's average GDP per capita rising to $5,395 in 2022, a 37.6% increase since 2015.

12. **$82,000 GDP per capita in Singapore**: Singapore remains ASEAN's wealthiest nation, with a GDP per capita of over $84,714.000 in December 2023, driven by finance, tech, and manufacturing.

Trade, investment, and finance

13. **$72 billion e-commerce market:** ASEAN's e-commerce market was valued at $72 billion in 2022, with continued growth expected as digital infrastructure expands.

14. **$26 billion BPO sector:** The Philippines' Business Process Outsourcing (BPO) sector generates over $26 billion annually, making it a global leader in the outsourcing industry.

15. **$3.4 trillion banking assets in ASEAN:** By 2019, the ASEAN banking sector managed over $3.4 trillion in total

assets, reflecting the region's strong financial infrastructure and its critical role in supporting trade and investment across member states.

Trade with Dialogue Partners

16. **$722 billion ASEAN-China trade:** Trade between ASEAN and China hit $722 billion in 2022, making China ASEAN's largest trading partner for the 13th consecutive year.

17. **$268 billion ASEAN-Japan trade:** ASEAN's trade with Japan reached $268 billion in 2022. Japan is one of ASEAN's most important economic partners, focusing on technology and infrastructure development.

18. **$420 billion ASEAN-United States trade:** Trade between ASEAN and the United States was valued at $420 billion in 2022, with the United States being one of ASEAN's top trading partners, especially in tech and manufacturing.

19. **$113 billion ASEAN-India trade:** ASEAN-India trade reached $113 billion in 2022, bolstered by sectors such as IT, pharmaceuticals, and services.

20. **$222 billion ASEAN-South Korea trade:** In 2022, ASEAN's trade with South Korea amounted to $122 billion, with key sectors including electronics, machinery, and shipbuilding.

21. **$116 billion ASEAN-Australia/New Zealand trade:** Trade between ASEAN and Australia-New Zealand (AANZFTA) reached $116 billion in 2022, with strong ties in education, agriculture, and energy.

22. **$295 billion ASEAN-European Union trade**: In 202, ASEAN's trade with the European Union stood at $295 billion, focusing on machinery, chemicals, and automotive exports.

23. **$15 billion ASEAN-Russia trade:** Trade between ASEAN and Russia reached $15 billion in 2022, with essential products being energy, machinery, and agricultural goods.

24. **$23 billion ASEAN-Canada trade**: ASEAN-Canada trade was valued at $23 billion in 2022, primarily in natural resources, aerospace, and services sectors.

25. **RCEP expected to generate $500 billion:** The Regional Comprehensive Economic Partnership (RCEP) agreement, signed in 2020, covers 30% of global GDP and is expected to create an additional $500 billion in trade among ASEAN and its partners by 2030.

Digital and tech economy

26. **$330 billion digital economy by 2025:** E-commerce, fintech, and digital trade growth are expected to drive the

growth of ASEAN's digital economy to $330 billion by 2025.

27. **80% internet penetration**: By 2022, internet penetration in ASEAN stood at 80%, with Indonesia, Malaysia, and Vietnam leading in digital adoption. More than 460 million people in Southeast Asia use the Internet.

28. **$25 billion ASEAN startup ecosystem:** As of 2022, ASEAN's startup ecosystem has attracted more than $25 billion in venture capital investments, with Singapore, Indonesia, and Vietnam being major hubs.

29. **460 million internet users in ASEAN:** By 2022, ASEAN had 460 million internet users, with 100 million coming online in the last three years. Of these, 370 million became digital consumers, driving e-commerce sales to USD 194 billion in 2022. Projections indicate this will grow to USD 363 billion by 2025 and could reach USD 1 trillion by 2030, highlighting the region's rapidly expanding digital economy.

30. **6 countries with 5G deployment:** By 2023, 5G networks have been deployed in 6 ASEAN countries - Indonesia, Malaysia, the Philippines, Singapore, Thailand, and Vietnam.

Infrastructure and connectivity

31. **$375 billion in regional trade by 2025:** ASEAN's regional trade is projected to hit $375 billion in 2025, driven by digital transformation, infrastructure development, and enhanced connectivity.

32. **$180 billion in BRI project commitments:** As of 2024, China's Belt and Road Initiative (BRI) has committed over $180 billion in ASEAN infrastructure projects, particularly transportation and energy.

33. **31 cities in the ASEAN Smart Cities Network:** By June 2024, 31 ASEAN cities will join the ASEAN Smart Cities Network (ASCN), focusing on urban sustainability and innovative city initiatives across the region.

34. **$15 billion Singapore-Kunming Rail Link (SKRL):** Major cross-border rail projects like the $6 billion Kunming-Laos railway are transforming ASEAN's connectivity. Upon completion in 2027, it is expected to boost trade by 15-20% within the region and reduce travel times across Southeast Asia.

Tourism and travel

35. **140 million tourists in 2019:** Pre-pandemic, ASEAN attracted about 140 million international tourists, with

Thailand, Malaysia, and Singapore among the top destinations.

36. **Tourism recovery projected at 80%:** ASEAN tourism is recovering in 2023, with projected international arrivals expected to reach 80% of pre-pandemic levels by year-end.

37. **12% tourism contribution to GDP:** Tourism accounts for an average of 12% of ASEAN's GDP, with countries like Thailand and Cambodia heavily reliant on this sector. It employs 42 million people in ASEAN.

38. **10.6 million Chinese tourists in ASEAN:** In 2023, over 10.6 million visitors arrived from China, making it the region's largest source of international tourists post-pandemic.

Energy and sustainability

39. **23% renewable energy goals:** ASEAN aims to achieve a 23% renewable energy share in its primary energy mix by 2025, driven by solar, wind, and hydro projects.

40. **60% energy demand growth by 2040:** ASEAN's energy demand is projected to increase by 60% by 2040, primarily due to industrialisation and urbanisation.

41. **85% of global palm oil production:** ASEAN, led by Indonesia and Malaysia, produces over 85% of the world's palm oil, a critical economic export for the region.

42. **70% of global natural rubber supply:** Around 70% of global natural rubber production originates from Thailand, Indonesia, and Malaysia.

Agriculture and food security

43. **40% of the world's rice supply**: With 48 million hectares under rice cultivation, Southeast Asia accounts for 40% of global rice exports as of 2022. Thailand and Vietnam are two of the world's largest rice exporters.

44. **787,000-ton rice reserve:** The ASEAN Plus Three Emergency Rice Reserve (APTERR), which is 787 tons and comprises 87,000 tonnes from the ASEAN member countries and 700,000 tonnes from the Plus Three countries, helps mitigate food shortages during crises.

45. **22% of global fish production**: ASEAN is a global leader in fisheries, accounting for over 22% of the world's fish production in 2022. The region's fisheries and aquaculture industries provide livelihoods for more than 10 million people.

Socio-cultural and development perspective

46. **$4 billion ASEAN Infrastructure Fund:** ASEAN launched the AIF to finance cross-border infrastructure projects, emphasising sustainable development.

47. **40% poverty reduction:** ASEAN's collective efforts have reduced extreme poverty from 47% in 1990 to less than 10% by 2022, significantly improving living standards across the region.

48. **30 core university members in the ASEAN University Network:** The ASEAN University Network (AUN) has grown to 30 members, facilitating higher education collaboration and benefiting many ASEAN students through academic exchange programs.

49. **41% of managerial positions held by women:** ASEAN countries have made strides in gender equality, with 41% of managerial positions held by women in the region in 2022.

50. **$4.3 million in humanitarian assistance:** Since its inception in 2011, the ASEAN Coordinating Centre for Humanitarian Assistance (AHA Centre) has mobilised $4.3 million in disaster relief across Southeast Asia, helping people recover from natural disasters and humanitarian crises.

The numbers presented in this chapter show the immense potential and dynamic nature of ASEAN as a region poised for continued growth and integration. The substantial population with a youthful demographic driving innovation positions ASEAN to harness its human capital for economic advancement in the coming years. As the fifth-largest economy globally, with strong intra-regional trade, ASEAN demonstrates a commitment to deepening economic ties among its member states, facilitated by initiatives like the ASEAN Free Trade Area and the elimination of tariffs and non-tariff barriers.

The anticipated growth of ASEAN's digital economy and e-commerce market illustrates the region's adaptability to technological advancements and the increasing significance of the digital landscape in driving economic resilience. Moreover, ambitious infrastructure projects, such as the Singapore-Kunming Rail Link (SKRL), are set to enhance connectivity and further boost trade within the region.

These statistics reflect ASEAN's robust framework for cooperation, economic integration, and social development, reinforcing its vital role on the international stage. The future looks promising, with continued efforts to address challenges and seize opportunities, ensuring that ASEAN remains a central player in promoting peace, stability, and prosperity in Southeast Asia and beyond. The numbers tell a compelling story of resilience and potential, charting a path forward for the region as it embraces an increasingly interconnected world.

"ASEAN's journey over the past five decades is filled with remarkable achievements and lesser-known stories that reflect its diversity and resilience. From its founding principles to its evolving role in the global arena, these fascinating facts capture the essence of ASEAN's unique identity and its profound impact on the region and the world."

Pushpanathan Sundram, Author

List of Abbreviations

1. AADMER: ASEAN Agreement on Disaster Management and Emergency Response
2. AANZFTA: ASEAN-Australia-New Zealand Free Trade Agreement
3. AAP-JRCC: ASEAN Action Plan on Joint Response to Climate Change
4. AATHP: ASEAN Agreement on Transboundary Haze Pollution
5. ABAC: ASEAN Business Advisory Council
6. ABIF: ASEAN Banking Integration Framework
7. ACCI: ASEAN Climate Change Initiative
8. ACCT: ASEAN Convention on Counter-Terrorism
9. ACE: ASEAN Centre for Energy
10. ACFTA: ASEAN-China Free Trade Agreement
11. ACIA:ASEAN Comprehensive Investment Agreement
12. ACCI: ASEAN Climate Change Initiative
13. ACCT: ASEAN Convention on Counter-Terrorism
14. ACSC: ASEAN Civil Society Conference
15. ACPHEED: ASEAN Centre for Public Health Emergencies and Emerging Diseases
16. ACTIP: ASEAN Convention Against Trafficking in Persons
17. ACW: ASEAN Committee on Women
18. ACRF: ASEAN Comprehensive Recovery Framework
19. ACSDSD: ASEAN Centre for Sustainable Development Studies and Dialogue
20. ADB: Asian Development Bank

21. ADMM: ASEAN Defence Ministers Meeting
22. AEC: ASEAN Economic Community
23. AFTA: ASEAN Free Trade Area
24. AFIF: ASEAN Financial Integration Framework
25. AFSRB: ASEAN Food Reserve Board
26. AHA Centre: ASEAN Coordinating Centre for Humanitarian Assistance
27. AHRD: ASEAN Human Rights Declaration
28. AICHR: ASEAN Intergovernmental Commission on Human Rights
29. AIF: ASEAN Infrastructure Fund
30. AIFS: ASEAN Integrated Food Security Framework
31. AIFTA: ASEAN India Free Trade Agreement
32. AIMD: ASEAN Integration Monitoring Directorate
33. AIPA: ASEAN Inter-Parliamentary Assembly
34. AJCEP: ASEAN-Japan Comprehensive Economic Partnership
35. AKFTA: ASEAN-Korea Free Trade Agreement
36. AUKUS: Australia-United Kingdom-United States trilateral security partnership
37. AMM: ASEAN Ministerial Meeting
38. AMRO: ASEAN+3 Macroeconomic Research Office
39. AOIP: ASEAN Outlook on the Indo-Pacific
40. APACE: ASEAN Plan of Action on Culture and Education
41. APAEC: ASEAN Plan of Action for Energy Cooperation
42. APF: ASEAN People's Forum

43. APHDA: ASEAN Post-2015 Health Development Agenda
44. APSC: ASEAN Political-Security Community
45. APT: ASEAN Plus Three (ASEAN+3)
46. APTERR: ASEAN Plus Three Emergency Rice Reserve
47. ARF: ASEAN Regional Forum
48. ASA: Association of Southeast Asia
49. ASCC: ASEAN Socio-Cultural Community
50. ASCCE: ASEAN-Singapore Cybersecurity Centre of Excellence
51. ASCN: ASEAN Smart Cities Network
52. ASCOE: ASEAN Committee on Education
53. ASEAN: Association of Southeast Asian Nations
54. ASEAN DERS: ASEAN Disaster Emergency Response Simulation Exercise
55. ASEAN-ISIS: ASEAN Institutes of Strategic and International Studies
56. ASEAN SEOM: ASEAN Senior Economic Officials Meeting
57. ASEAN SOM: ASEAN Senior Officials Meeting
58. ASEAN COCI: ASEAN Committee on Culture and Information
59. ASW: ASEAN Single Window
60. ATIGA: ASEAN Trade in Goods Agreement
61. ATISA: ASEAN Trade in Services Agreement
62. AUN: ASEAN University Network
63. AWGCC: ASEAN Working Group on Climate Change
64. AZEC: Asia Zero Emission Community

65. BRICS: Brazil, Russia, India, China, South Africa (Inter-governmental Organisation)
66. BRI: Belt and Road Initiative
67. CERTs: Computer Emergency Response Teams
68. CMLV: Cambodia, Myanmar, Laos, and Vietnam
69. CMIM: Chiang Mai Initiative Multilateralisation
70. COC: Code of Conduct in the South China Sea
71. CPTPP: Comprehensive and Progressive Agreement for Trans-Pacific Partnership
72. CPR: Committee of Permanent Representatives
73. CSP: Comprehensive Strategic Partnership
74. DOC: Declaration on the Conduct of Parties in the South China Sea
75. DSG: Deputy Secretary-General
76. EAS: East Asia Summit
77. ERIA: Economic Research Institute of ASEAN and East Asia
78. EU: European Union
79. FAO: Food and Agriculture Organisation
80. FDI: Foreign Direct Investment
81. FTA: Free Trade Agreement
82. GEF: Global Environment Facility
83. IAI: Initiative for ASEAN Integration
84. ICJ: International Court of Justice
85. IMF: International Monetary Fund
86. IPEF: Indo-Pacific Economic Framework
87. IPCC: Intergovernmental Panel on Climate Change
88. IPR: Intellectual Property Rights

89. MAPHILINDO: Malaysia, Philippines, and Indonesia Confederation
90. MPAC: Master Plan on ASEAN Connectivity
91. NCDs: Non-Communicable Diseases
92. NDCs: Nationally Determined Contributions
93. NTBs: Non-Tariff Barriers
94. NTMs: Non-Tariff Measures
95. PCA: Partnership and Cooperation Agreement
96. Quad: Quadrilateral Security Dialogue (Australia, India, Japan and United States)
97. RCEP: Regional Comprehensive Economic Partnership
98. SCP: Sustainable Consumption and Production
99. SEANWFZ: Southeast Asia Nuclear-Weapon-Free Zone
100. SEATO: Southeast Asia Treaty Organisation
101. SG: Secretary-General
102. SMEs: Small and Medium Enterprises
103. SPA-FS: Strategic Plan of Action on Food Security
104. TAC: Treaty of Amity and Cooperation
105. TBT: Technical Barriers to Trade
106. TVET: Technical and Vocational Education and Training
107. UNDP: United Nations Development Programme
108. UNDRR: United Nations Office for Disaster Risk Reduction
109. UNEP: United Nations Environmental Program
110. UNESCO: United Nations Educational, Scientific and Cultural Organisation

111. UN OCHA: United Nations Office for the Coordination of Humanitarian Affairs
112. UNODC: United Nations Office on Drugs and Crime
113. UN SDGs: United Nations Sustainable Development Goals
114. WHO: World Health Organisation
115. WTO: World Trade Organisation
116. WTO TFA: WTO Trade Facilitation Agreement
117. ZOPFAN: Zone of Peace, Freedom, and Neutrality

Index

A

B

C

D

E

T

U

V

W

Z

The Author

Dr Pushpanathan Sundram, a C-suite executive, industry leader and a leading expert on ASEAN affairs with over 30 years of experience in business, trade association management, public policy, economic integration, and regional diplomacy, has held several pivotal roles in ASEAN. This includes serving as the youngest and first professionally recruited Deputy Secretary-General (Deputy Minister) of ASEAN for the ASEAN Economic Community (AEC) from 2009 to 2011. He was instrumental in driving economic integration, shaping trade policies, and drafting key frameworks such as the AEC Blueprint and the Master Plan on ASEAN Connectivity 2009-2015. He has assisted in advancing ASEAN's regional security, economic cooperation, and external relations with major powers, contributing to peace, stability, and growth in Southeast Asia. Recognised for his contributions, he has received prestigious awards, including Cambodia's Sahakmetrei Medal (Commander Class) and the inaugural Outstanding Alumni Award from the Lee Kuan Yew School of Public Policy, National University of Singapore. A Visiting Fellow with the School of Public Policy, Chiang Mai University, he has published extensively and continues to shape academic and policy discourse on ASEAN, regional diplomacy and public policy.

www.ingramcontent.com/pod-product-compliance
Ingram Content Group UK Ltd.
Pitfield, Milton Keynes, MK11 3LW, UK
UKHW041633190726
13854UKWH00006B/2479